WHEN'S HAPPY HOUR?

ALSO BY BETCHES

I Had a Nice Time and Other Lies . . .

Nice Is Just a Place in France

betches

WHEN'S HAPPY HOUR?

WORK HARD SO YOU CAN HARDLY WORK

G

GALLERY BOOKS

New York   London   Toronto   Sydney   New Delhi

G

Gallery Books
An Imprint of Simon & Schuster, Inc.
1230 Avenue of the Americas
New York, NY 10020

First Gallery Books hardcover edition October 2018

GALLERY BOOKS and colophon are registered trademarks of Simon & Schuster, Inc.

For information about special discounts for bulk purchases, please contact Simon & Schuster Special Sales at 1-866-506-1949 or business@simonandschuster.com.

The Simon & Schuster Speakers Bureau can bring authors to your live event. For more information or to book an event, contact the Simon & Schuster Speakers Bureau at 1-866-248-3049 or visit our website at www.simonspeakers.com.

Art by Kenzie Szymarek

Manufactured in the United States of America

10 9 8 7 6 5 4 3 2 1

Library of Congress Cataloging-in-Publication Data

Names: Betches (Group)
Title: When's happy hour? : work hard so you can hardly work / The Betches.
Other titles: When is happy hour?
Description: New York : Gallery Books, [2018]
Identifiers: LCCN 2018023019| ISBN 9781501198984 (hardcover) |
   ISBN 9781501198991 (trade pbk.) | ISBN 9781501199004 (ebook)
Subjects: LCSH: Women-Employment. | Sex role in the work environment.
Classification: LCC HD6053 .B478 2018 | DDC 650.1082–dc23
LC record available at https://lccn.loc.gov/2018023019.

ISBN 978-1-5011-9898-4
ISBN 978-1-5011- 9900-4 (ebook)

To all the betches out there
who sometimes feel like they want to be CEO and then
other times feel like they want to stay home and bake cookies.

Contents

WHEN'S HAPPY HOUR?

Introduction
NICE TO E-MEET YOU

It's the second Tuesday in February; you're in the bathroom stall in your office building, and you're crying. Like really embarrassingly crying. Worse than Kim Kardashian after five vials of filler. It's not because someone just died; no, it's so much lamer than that. You just don't want to go back to your desk. Everyone at work sucks, your boss is mean, the girls at work are petty, the coworker who ghosted you just got a promotion, and the only good thing your job has going for it are the office snacks. You ask yourself, *Can I get away with staying in here until 5:00 p.m.? I literally do not care about this job, why the fuck am I here?*

You're asking yourself the wrong question. Deep down, what you're really asking yourself is: *Why do I even care about this job? Does my career even matter?* If you just murmured "no" under your breath, put this book down and head over to bachelor.com/casting. Seriously, no judgment; if anything, we fully respect your willingness to either spend your trust fund or to carry credit card debt so brazenly.

But barring future bachelorettes, the truth is, it really doesn't matter what you do . . . to anyone but you. We're all a little bit narcissistic and self-centered here (heads up, Peace Corps volunteer-types and the extremely PC crowd should probably see yourselves out), so if you truly care about yourself as a person, then yes, without question you should care about your career. Valuing yourself means, at least in part, that you should automatically invest *a lot* of thought in what you spend your waking hours doing and thinking about.

We're going to assume that you're the type of person who already cares a lot about your career, simply based on the fact that you opened a "career book" (we know, "career book" sounds so boring, which is exactly the problem). But let's say this is your first time dabbling in noncomplacency. This book will show you why it's actually worth it to invest time and energy into your own future so you don't end up with a life that just happened to you, instead of one you created for yourself.

We all have that friend who seems to float around for her entire twenties without any real direction and no apparent desire to change that. We also all know the friend who dutifully attends her job every day but literally couldn't care less about what she actually does beyond mining office gossip about who's hooking up with whom. To each their own.

But as entertaining and comfortable as it is to never invest too much in your advancement—no one's claiming to enjoy the heart palpitations that come along with a high-stakes work email—there's something much bleaker about the thought of spending eight to ten hours a day working for results that are less important to you than those of a *Watch What Happens Live* poll. (Though, yes, we do feel strongly that LuAnn is going to change her ways after rehab.)

We admit that not everyone is cut out to be an executive or thrive in an environment in which money is prized as the gold standard of human worth (which, let's be real, is true of most professions in America). TBH that is *so* not for us, either. We run a company whose name is derived from the word *bitches*, so you know our office is not exactly the trading desk at Goldman Sachs. Which is why we're the perfect people to tell you that "passionately pursuing your career" doesn't have to mean dealing with lame, petty bullshit typically associated with "career achievement."

To be serious for like, a hot sec, we also want to start with a caveat and a disclaimer that what we discuss in this "career book" is not going to make sense for everyone. First of all, if you're the type of person who has never really enjoyed or felt interest in working but have always wanted kids and genuinely feel fulfilled in taking care of your home, then this book is really not going to apply to you. But you should read it anyway, because it's funny, and you're probably bored out of your mind chasing toddlers around your kitchen. For real, though, we have a ton of respect for women who genuinely want to be full-time mothers and have the resources to do that. Plus, your kids will never get to be all like, "You didn't even raise us, the nanny did!" We feel strongly that if that is what you want, then that is exactly what you should do.

We also realize that all three of us come from specific, pretty privileged backgrounds (upper middle class, college educated, white, able-bodied) and some of our advice cannot be taken by women in situations that are unlike our own. We also realize that we have a unique situation of career experience in the start-up world and that literally everyone's personal situation is different. We're going to be making generalizations throughout this book that may not sit well with everyone, and—for once in our lives—we truly mean no offense. Enjoy this book for its humor, reap the benefits of whatever advice might speak to you, and leave the rest behind. Okay, now back to our very strong and important opinions.

A lot of think pieces have been thought-pieced about the internet and millennials' usage of it, but one gift that it has for sure given each of us is the ability to be our own "brands" and to start our own initiatives without the barriers of previous decades. It's now easier than ever for young people to build our own paths. And we don't just mean using the internet to blast out your new coconut-pepita raw ball recipe to two hundred people. We mean taking online courses to invest in yourself if you hate what you do and want a career change, or reaching out to people who would otherwise be inaccessible strangers for advice or new career opportunities. Not to sound lame or idealistic, but the internet contains so many more tools to help us do what we want to do and become what we want to be. So if you're still the person who literally doesn't care at all what you make of your life, the only thing stopping you from attempting to make changes at this point is laziness. We get it, we also just *need* to rewatch the entire series of *The OC* again.

For anyone who's been following Betches from the beginning, you may recall that we used to ruthlessly mock people who tried in earnest to achieve anything or who worked hard in pursuit of their passions. "Not doing work" was literally one of the major pillars we wrote about in our first book, *Nice Is Just a Place in France: How to Win at Basically Everything*. Since then, we've grown up and had a change of heart. Suddenly, not giving a shit about anything doesn't seem so cool anymore. Once we realized that working and pursuing a goal was nothing like we had been taught in school (see, school is the problem here, not us), our perspective drastically changed. We realized that a "career" doesn't have to be this anxiety-inducing, dreadful, boring, cookie-cutter thing. If you set yourself up to do something that motivates you and that you actually find fulfilling, your career *can* be as empowering as the motivational posters have been saying all along. Doesn't that sound like it's worth giving a shit about?

WHO ARE WE AND WHY YOU SHOULD LISTEN TO US

It's probably time that we introduce ourselves. We're Aleen, Jordana, and Sami, the cofounders of Betches Media (which was Betches, also Betches Love This, also Betches Love This Site, for the truly OG readers) and the coauthors of this incredible book you're currently half reading while streaming Netflix.

The three of us met in elementary school in Roslyn, New York. Aleen's and Jordana's moms were both ob-gyns and introduced the two at their fifth-grade graduation. Meanwhile, Aleen and Sami lived around the corner from each other and naturally sat together on the bus in an attempt to soak up each other's awesomeness (without the shooters, this was like, fifth grade). And as we grew older, we only got closer. We were in a lot of the same classes, had a lot of the same friends, and all laughed at the same weird shit.

Anecdote from
Eighth-Grade English Class

Jordana and Aleen will not stop talking throughout class.

Mrs. Zaney*: I will move the two of you if you do not stop talking this instant!

Jordana and Aleen immediately continue talking.

Mrs. Zaney: *That's it!* Aleen, I'm moving you across the room. . . . Go sit behind Sami.

Aleen, Jordana, and Sami all smile at each other.

Fast-forward to like, going to college and shit. Yes, we all went to Cornell, ever heard of it? And lived together our senior year. Jordana was a policy major, Aleen was premed, and Sami studied industrial labor relations and some other Hogwartsy-sounding words. The point of telling you this is that *none of us studied business* but that didn't stop us from having a really good idea one very cold and boring February night.

First we started wondering:

- What's with all this glorified bro shit flying around everywhere?

---

* Name changed, but you know who you are.

- The things our friends do and say on a daily basis are highly offensive but also insanely hysterical.
- But really, how come guys can act like assholes and do what they want as long as they call themselves *bros* and the only name girls can call themselves is *bitch* or maybe the slightly less aggressive *beyotch*?
- We're like, way funnier than a lot of these sites people are reading.
- What if we gave girls a word to be the counterpart to the bro that we can be proud to call ourselves? And then we can say what girls are *actually* thinking but they're afraid to say out loud.

Friendly and fucked-up reminder: This was early 2011, before Instagram was even a thing.

That's where Betches started. We thought that the word should be *betch*, because it's the word *bitch* pronounced with vocal fry, which was the way everyone around us would say it—i.e., "You're such a behhhhhtch; I love you." We were inspired by all the satirical lists that were trending at the time (Stuff White People Like, etc.), so we figured that was the best way to portray and make fun of the betch lifestyle without sounding like total haters. After all, we were still writing about ourselves.

So we stayed up all night writing the first five articles of the Betch List:

1. "Talking Shit"

2. "Not Keeping Up with the News"

3. "Studying Abroad"

4. "Mobile Uploads"

5. "Diets"

The rest is viral history.

We chose to remain anonymous at the beginning primarily because we really wanted to get jobs at the end of the semester but also because it was kind of fun and Gossip Girly. The coolest and most surprising thing that came out of the anonymity was that it let the content go viral beyond the bubble we lived in. Girls from the Midwest and the South were freaking out, commenting things like "Omg who is writing this it sounds like my best friend wrote this" and "AMANDA IS THAT FUCKING YOU!?"

At that point, we knew we were onto something.

SO WHERE TF ARE YOU RIGHT NOW?

Can't you just like, check our LinkedIn? Ugh, okay. So we have a real office now and everything. We have eighteen full-time employees as of this writing. We've never taken investment in the company, meaning we've been putting the profit back into the business and we still own the whole thing. (If you take investors' money to grow your business, they want a say in how you run it.) We have two *New York Times*–bestselling books, a growing network of podcasts, a popular e-commerce site, and we've grown to an audience of more than six million on Instagram alone. There's also a lot more to plug but we just don't have time for that. Oh and we even have retirement accounts. We're like, total grown-ups.

HOW DID WE GET HERE?

Persistence and taking a page out of Ross Geller's book: PIVOT. PIVOOOOT.

Getting ahead in this business never really came easy to us. We didn't "know people." In fact, since we all came from the same town and went to the same college, we all knew the same fucking people, which really didn't help our "network." When we started, our network literally consisted of Sami's business-savvy grandfather, Aleen's tech-savvy dad, and Jordana's lawyer uncle. It legitimately sounded like the beginning of a terrible dad joke.

On top of that, all three of us have super-creative personalities, which doesn't usually come with being good at networking. For example, when we finally decided to get a small office in a WeWork in 2014, we convinced ourselves that it would be a good investment because we'd be forced to meet other people. Yet, any time we saw there was an event happening on our floor, we made sure to ditch early and go out the back elevators. And then we went to have drinks together, alone.

While the above paragraph makes us sound like reclusive loners, there's an important upside to never wanting to meet anyone new. Even though we were "antisocial" in the networking sense, being able to focus on honing our craft definitely got us to where we are now. (We'll let you make comparisons to Steve Jobs on your own.) We kept focusing on the company's content, while also simply/not so simply trying to figure out how said company was going to make money.

The other core idea that got us to where we are today, and that continues to drive us forward, is the subconscious decision to not hold on to the "glory days," which allows us to constantly change our course of action. Pivoting is something we do on the reg. It's become second nature. Holding on to old shit that doesn't work is like Lindsay Lohan reposting an October 3 meme on October 3rd. Ugh.

Just like a person who still talks about how cool she was in high school probably hates her life right now, a company also has to evolve to be successful or it'll get left behind. Behind every company is just a bunch of people living in a fast-paced society trying to make some fucking decisions so they don't become irrelevant or, worse, poor.

To use ourselves as a very general example (listen, we're going to use ourselves as an example through the whole book, so get used to it): Seven years ago, we were literally asshole kids who'd just graduated college and were convinced that we knew the answers to everything. We said whatever we wanted and got away with it because our audience was down with everything we did. Most notably, we never really called ourselves feminists. At the time, the term *feminist* seemed to us to mean being a man-hating extremist, and as twenty-two-year-olds we couldn't make ourselves care about anything that much except ourselves.

But time went on and the stereotype of "feminism" began to change. We realized that we were wrong about what feminism really meant, and that duh, of course we were feminists, and proud to be. Not only did we run a business with a mission centered on female empowerment, where the vast majority of our employees and audience were women; we also realized that we could truly have an impact on advancing female equality. It dawned on us what an important opportunity this was.

This realization was not only very meaningful for us as people but also for the company, because it helped us realize that we actually had a mission beyond creating funny content (every company needs a mission—not just nonprofits like we thought when we were twenty-two—but we'll get to that later).

Over time, we realized that the way we usually described our company was actually building the foundation of our current mission. Like, "saying whatever the fuck we wanted" grew to be "saying the things other people are too afraid to say out loud."

"Talking shit" became "using humor to observe and call out the ridiculous behaviors we see in the world."

And every single one of our references and questionable word choices became "speaking to women the way they speak to each other."

And while you might be thinking, *Guys, this is just marketing*—you're right, but that's not the point. With all the time we spent growing this business and experiencing what it's like to run a company, we learned so much about ourselves and the Betches Media you know today.

As three women who just thought we were being funny and doing what we loved, the moment we realized that the company we'd created actually had a voice that could make a difference in our fight for equality was empowering.

SO WHY READ THIS BOOK?

Serious disclaimer: Even though we're about to give you a lot of career and entrepreneurial advice, we've had a very sheltered experience when it comes to understanding the workforce because we've only really done this one thing. We don't claim to know everything. Everyone is just using the cards they've been dealt, and not everyone can afford the luxury of getting to decide what they want to do with their lives. We fully realize and feel grateful for the gift of being in this position. Namaste.

That said, we still have advice to offer, and that advice is based on our own experience. While it is singular in the sense that Betches Media is all that we know firsthand, the limit does not exist for all the crazy shit that's happened to us and lessons we've learned along the way. Also, this includes all the things we've heard about from our friends and people we've surveyed in the course of writing this book. We've made so many mistakes and played by just as many rules as we've broken. We've failed, we've succeeded, we were lazy, we were stressed, and we wanted to give up. But we also worked really hard to get where we are despite the fact that one of the tenets of betchiness is getting by while doing the absolute minimum. Like we mentioned, we changed. Really mature and shit. So you're getting the benefit of that experience without having to live it, which is pretty efficient.

And one other thing you might get out of this book? A fucking clue.

During our years working with female millennials, we, alongside everyone else and their mothers, noticed that millennials don't want to do much. We're known as an entitled generation, and for a lot of us, that's true. But as entitled as some of us may appear, the truth is that we witness firsthand every day how hardworking and driven millennials can be when they want to achieve something.

So if you need guidance for situations like: *What should I ask in a first-round interview? How do I ask for a raise? How do I work crop tops into my office wardrobe? And why won't the IT guy I hooked up with at the holiday party help me figure out how to connect to the fucking printer?* If you've ever struggled with a workplace romance gone bad, tried to figure out how to get promoted, or found yourself so bored at work that you calculated the seconds left until happy hour, you should definitely keep reading.

Warmest regards, sincerely, and please advise,

Aleen, Jordana, and Samantha

1.
LOOKING FORWARD TO CATCHING UP!

A History of Women in the Workforce

Before we can really talk about women at work, we have to talk about the F-word: feminism. If you're reading this book, chances are you can't remember a time when feminism wasn't a topic of conversation, for better or worse. For many people, feminism has always had a positive connotation and held a well-defined place in their belief system. We wish we could say that we were three of these people. The truth is, that for much of our early lives, we learned to associate feminism with many of the negative things that defensive old white men wanted us to associate it with, such as wanting to dominate men rather than date them, wanting to look and dress like men while covering up our femininity, and generally just looking for a banner cause to allow us to take our anger out on men. While we could always agree that women deserved to be equal to men—and that all people deserve to be equal—we had difficulty owning the word *feminism*.

And we don't think we're the only ones who felt this way. Remember when Emma Watson gave a speech at the UN where she openly declared herself a feminist and a bunch of people were like, "Wow, she is totally avada-kadavra'ing my anti-feminist vibe." We're happy to say that Emma, among other people and events, have helped us evolve and get an actual clue about the true level of inequality that persists when we don't take a stand. We've seen over time how feminism has gone from being a third rail for many women to becoming a defining cause for them, and how a lot of the negativity we formerly associated it with has been removed. Praise be.

> I think the word is really difficult because it seems to inherently address a preferential treatment of the feminine over the masculine because it has the feminine in the word, and I think that's a real oversight and misunderstanding. This isn't just girls are better than boys, boys are better than girls. This is just everyone deserves a fair chance.
>
> —Emma Watson

While it may sometimes feel like feminism has always been a given and that these days you can't even tweet criticism of the female lead in your favorite TV show without being accused of "not supporting women," the reality is that feminism is relatively historically new. Depending on how old you are, it's possible that your very own grandmother or great-grandmother wasn't allowed to vote for a substantial portion of her life. Also, while women in the first world may have progressed all the way to fighting for nipple freedom on Instagram, the truth is that feminism is still not that popular yet in the rest of the world. For example, women earned the right to drive in Saudi Arabia just in this past year. Big strides. We wish we meant that sarcastically.

The world may have a long way to go, but lucky for those of us living in America in 2018, many of the negative connotations of feminism (bra-burning, man-hating, and the rest of men's rights activists' greatest hits) have been stripped away. Celebrities, politicians, business owners, and other powerful people no longer avoid the question "are you a feminist?" like someone just asked about a past DUI. At the same time, there are still a lot of women who hold negative associations about feminists, and for that reason we have a long way to go before all of society comes around to the idea that we should treat human beings as if they deserve equal rights, regardless of their genitalia or any other physical characteristic. Before we get into the modern-day struggles of betches in the workforce, let's take a look at where we came from, and how we've earned the privilege of joining said workforce while still earning at least 30 percent less than men.

PRE-ENLIGHTENMENT

For the vast majority of world history, women had no choice but to stay at home, take care of the kids, and cook fattening, carb-loaded meals for their families. And they couldn't even upload pics of them to Instagram. Back when humans were hunter-gatherers, women had jobs, obviously, but those jobs were to cook the animals that the men went out and hunted. This kind of economic separation of the sexes was fairly efficient, as women are physically smaller than men (usually). And while a skinny arm might look good in pics, it made spearing a fish to death hard. Sadly, this history led to the tired-as-fuck idea that frat bros and angry men like to proclaim: a woman's place is in the kitchen.

But mankind no longer survives by hunting and gathering. Don't get us wrong, the chicken in our fast-casual salads would have way fewer GMOs if we did. Thanks to technology, your physical size and ability to kill a deer no longer determines your role in the workforce. Over time, society got a few glow-ups and eventually became all industrialized and shit, and as a result, there have been a number of important milestones for women in the workforce. Let's examine a few of them and how they've contributed to the fact that you're reading this book and not cleaning your husband's loincloth while he goes out and wrestles a goat for lunch.

AGE OF ENLIGHTENMENT (EIGHTEENTH CENTURY)

Back in the Middle Ages, a common misconception was that women were dumber than men and therefore couldn't think at a high enough level to be allowed to enter the workforce. Enter the Enlightenment. Once everyone took a break from dying of the plague and had some free time on their hands, that opinion started to change. We know, we know. The guy in the cubicle next to you just asked who Columbus Day is a celebration of, yet there was a time when it was not common knowledge that women are just as smart, if not smarter, than men.

Some early feminists began to emerge around the mid-seventeenth to early eighteenth centuries, which finally got the ball rolling for us. The biggest celeb among these women is Mary Wollstonecraft, who wrote in 1792 that women weren't inferior

> I say, it's the women today, smarter than the men in every way.
>
> —Grateful Dead

in the mind, just in education. True. Despite that, betches still weren't even admitted to most Ivy League schools until the late 1960s, which shows you how intent men were on keeping women out of their territory. Good for when you're too hungover to go to biology lecture, bad for women's liberation.

INDUSTRIAL REVOLUTION (NINETEENTH CENTURY)

The Industrial Revolution, besides being a great metaphor for *The Puppy Who Lost Its Way*, was the first time women really started to leave their homes en masse. But obviously, shit was still not pleasant. Forget maternity leave, dangerous factories tended to hire women more because they were known for enduring harsher conditions and accepting lower pay without bitching about it. Women made up as much as one-third of the factory labor force, and working-class women really had to get out there in case their husbands got injured, since disability insurance was like, not a thing. While a working environment where your boss doesn't give a shit if your hand gets cut off is not exactly ideal, the Industrial Revolution gave women what they had been waiting thousands of years for: an opportunity to get out of the house and into the economy.

FIRST WAVE FEMINISM AND WOMEN'S SUFFRAGE (NINETEENTH CENTURY TO EARLY TWENTIETH CENTURY)

The term *first wave feminism* refers to the first major feminist movement, which (according to Wikipedia) was mainly focused on legal issues and getting the right to vote. Unlike your friend who needs to be bribed with an "I Voted" sticker to get off her ass and vote, women at this time were pretty into the idea of spending Tuesdays in a long-ass line at the polling place. And who can blame them. Both reality and

> *No man is good enough to govern any woman without her consent.*
>
> —Susan B. Anthony

The Handmaid's Tale have taught us how terrible things can be when men get to pass all the laws without our having a say in them.

If you ever feel like women have been coasting for centuries now, think again. Women weren't even given shared ownership of their own children until the 1840s, when states began passing Married Women's Property Acts. And regarding the whole right-to-vote thing, this shit did not come easy. The movement kicked off at the Seneca Falls ~~Festival~~ Convention, where the biggest feminist influencers of the day gathered to discuss political, social, and religious rights of women at the

> *Jimmy Dugan:* Chicken shit, Dottie, if you want to go back home to Oregon and make a hundred babies, great—I'm in no position to tell anyone how to live. But sneaking out like this—quitting—you'll regret it for the rest of your life. Baseball is what gets inside you. It's what lights you up; you can't deny that.
>
> *Dottie Hinson:* It just got too hard.
>
> *Jimmy Dugan:* It's supposed to be hard. If it wasn't hard, everyone would do it. The hard . . . is what makes it great.
>
> —A League of Their Own

time. Some major headliners of the era were Susan B. Anthony, Elizabeth Cady Stanton (it's Kady), Margaret Fuller, Sojourner Truth, Harriet Beecher Stowe, and all their suggested follows on Insta. This era was the first time that women had access to a lot of things we needed to get to where we are today, such as higher education, public office, and even the right to the same grounds for divorce as men. But the most significant change brought about by the first wave movement was the passage of the Nineteenth Amendment in 1920, which finally gave women the right to vote. So don't take that sticker for granted, k?

WORLD WAR II (1940s)

World War II—in addition to being a total shit show for the whole world—was when work really started to pick up for women everywhere. With men at war, millions of women of all classes were encouraged to get jobs and found out that they actually liked working. Kind of like that time you complained about having to do travel soccer after school but then you actually went and found out you were amazing at soccer. When the guys returned from war, women were encouraged to go back to life in the home, but by that point we'd had a taste of independence and were no longer tolerating not having a choice in the matter. A good number of us decided that life could be more than washing our husbands' dirty clothes. We decided to stay.

SECOND WAVE FEMINISM AND THE CIVIL RIGHTS ACT OF 1964

While first wave feminism was all about voting and legal rights, second wave feminism was about achieving equality in employment, workplace rights, reproductive rights, education, and advancing women socially through changes in dress, sexual freedom, and of course, the right to burn our bras.

For most of the twentieth century in America, women who wanted to or had to work were relegated to being nurses, teachers, or "hawkers," a.k.a. women who sell shit at the market like they did in that *Game of Thrones* episode where the king tries to get Daenerys Targaryen poisoned. Women struggled to be treated as equals or get hired in a ton of fields that men were dominant in (so like, every field). While this may not have been a huge problem in decades prior because women seemed like they were cool with being stay-at-home moms, the 1960s was when everything started to change. A major influence on women wanting to get out of the home and into the workforce was the publication of *The Feminine Mystique* by Betty Friedan, who popularized the idea that women were dissatisfied in their cute little nuclear family homes and were ready to find fulfillment through their careers. This book is credited for sparking the beginning of second wave feminism and changing the makeup of the American workforce from then on.

One of the biggest victories to come out of this time was the Civil Rights Act of 1964, which outlawed discrimination in the workforce based on race, color, religion, sex, or national origin. This law was a milestone for women (and like, people in general) because, while they had always been allowed to have some jobs, it made it illegal for men to not hire us just because we had vaginas. After that, it became apparent that if we were going to now be competing with men for jobs on an equal playing field, we would need to get the skills and education to do so.

> *Man is defined as a human being, and a woman, as a female. Whenever she behaves as a human being she is said to imitate the male.*
>
> —Simone de Beauvoir

As a result, women flooded both colleges and grad schools in the 1970s in record numbers. Women discovered they were naturals at getting paid to win arguments, and now there are even more women enrolled in law schools than men.

But as has been the case with every moment of female advancement, there was still some backlash against women gaining higher education. Some women were criticized for being in college only to find a husband. Imagine that! Like when your friend Ashley got engaged right after college and stopped working and you were thinking, "Why did you even take advanced calculus, Ashley??" The "MRS" degree is still unfortunately a thing but like, way less socially acceptable.

> I have yet to hear a man ask for advice on how to combine marriage and a career.
>
> —Gloria Steinem

College is expensive; don't let those textbooks that you sold back to your school for cash to buy weed go to waste.

MODERN DAY AND THE #METOO MOVEMENT

The fight continues. Think of the trend of women's advancement like the career of Peggy Olson in *Mad Men*: she started as a lowly secretary being sexually harassed by her bosses, and she ended up as copy chief and in a romantic relationship with her coworker. In other words, she made a ton of progress and suffered a lot to gain some power, but she's still not the top boss, and she's still largely defined by her relationship status. A classic women's lib fairy tale.

We can't talk about the state of modern-day feminism without addressing some of today's most important trending topics, #MeToo and #TimesUp. It may have appeared for a while that second wave feminism took care of granting us equality in the workforce, but many of the revelations of 2018 held up a giant mirror (and it was *not* a skinny one) to the fact that massive power imbalances still exist in many workplaces and industries, effectively undermining the equality afforded to women by law. The stories that have come out of the #MeToo movement have sent a powerful message that for all practical purposes, many industries are still heavily male-run and are therefore built to enable a lot of men's unsavory and illegal behavior. And what we mean by that is that some of these assholes are still acting like Peggy Olson's bosses in Season One; they just cover it up a little better.

The truth is that we're going to have a hard time reversing this latent inequality while men are still disproportionately running things. As anyone trying to get a job will tell you, a lot of times workers are simply at the mercy of their employers, and if said employer is an asshole who is emotionally disturbed enough to use his power to inappropriately touch, harass, and abuse you, then dealing with that dynamic may become an unwritten part of your job description. Which is exactly why #MeToo and #TimesUp are so necessary: to stop this behavior on a cultural level, as clearly the actual law isn't always enough of a deterrent. This movement has taught us that no matter how many sexual harassment policies or trainings a company has, at the end of the day it comes down to the men themselves to change their own beliefs and behavior, whether that's because they genuinely feel it's wrong to treat women this way or because they feel social pressure to act appropriately. We can't say we really give a shit what motivates them to act better, as long they stop taking out their inadequacies and insecurities on the women over whose lives they wield power.

At the same time, more women need to advance in order to change the inequality at the top and change the culture of male power and abuse. And while 2018 may be literally the first year in all of human history that being a rich white man hasn't landed you definitively at the top of every situation imaginable, we're still very far away from complete equality of earning and opportunity, especially for women of color. Despite higher rates of education, the Census Bureau calculates that the median white woman in the United States makes approximately 80 cents for every dollar paid to the median man. The number is even lower for women of color, which can be as low as 64 cents for African American women and 56 cents for Hispanic women. We have a sneaking suspicion that the same forces that liberate and elevate women through the #MeToo movement will eventually help improve those statistics.

At the same time, we don't want to discredit all the strides we've made so far. Female empowerment is now a mainstream conversation and it has become trendy for women to be in leadership positions. There are more female CEOs than there have ever been and more companies offering policies that benefit women, like paid family leave and in-house childcare. If we're going to live in a world that requires us to work forty-plus hours a week, at least we live in a time when wearing pants to the office isn't frowned upon and high heels are a personal choice. What a privilege.

The #MeToo era is still playing out and we can't know just yet what the long-term impact will be, but we do know that in the grand scheme of things, women have come a long way since our only option was to find a husband and take care of the home he pays for. Now that society has finally granted women some real opportunity to self-actualize and run our own lives in a way that was historically not socially acceptable, we'll be damned if we waste our lives helping men secure their legacies while we clean up their messes. They say that behind every great man is a great woman, but fuck that: the great man standing next to us can hold our purses while we give quarterly earnings reports, since we're the goddamn CEOs.

Inspirational Career Betch: Marie Curie

I have frequently been questioned, especially by women, of how I could reconcile family life with a scientific career. Well, it has not been easy.
—Marie Curie

Marie Curie discovered radium and was the first woman to ever win a Nobel Prize and the first *person* to ever win two of them. Not bad for a woman born in 1867 who wasn't even allowed to go to college because of her gender. Marie had to go to an underground "floating" school where she could learn in private. Like, imagine not even being allowed to take AP chemistry in high school and then fucking discovering radium. Makes for a way better high school reunion story than inventing Post-its. She took a governess job (a.k.a. fancy-ass term for a nanny) to earn money, and on the side she secretly studied chemistry, physics, and math. Meanwhile, the only thing most people learn while babysitting is how to catch up on Instagram stalking. Marie knew her shit so well that her scientist husband quit his own work to help her discover radium. She's a great example of perseverance of a passion—a side hustle will pay off eventually—and inspiration to always stay motivated despite the odds against you.

- -
TL;DR
- -

Women have had to overcome a lot of adversity in the workforce to get to the place we are at now. Since we had limited experience actually working outside our homes, it makes sense that it'll take us a while to catch up to the practices and mindsets that have been ingrained in men for years. You can't know where you're going if you don't know where you came from, which is why understanding the history of women in the workforce is so important for ensuring change in the future.

Hey, Betches,

I've been working in my current job for three and a half years. I asked for a raise and promotion a year ago and it was well received by my boss until he changed his mind and decided that I still had "growing" to do in order to fill the bigger role and salary. I absorbed another team member, which I am thankful for, experience-wise, but I felt taken advantage of, especially when this matter escalated to HR, who confirmed my suspicions of gender discrimination. My boss had rewarded my direct report (a male) by growing him $10,000 and three title levels and also promoted the only other male on my team to my level, sans any growth in responsibilities or any direct reports, which employees at this level typically have.

HR pulled the plug on disciplining my boss and gave me a supervised meeting where I was told that I need to speak less (literally too opinionated in meetings and he is "uncomfortable" with that) and that my writing was in need of improvement. I have yet to receive a single example of my work that wasn't up to snuff, despite multiple requests for feedback.

The dust has since settled, and I was able to ride out the last twelve months to receive my master's degree, which was fully covered by said employer. Now I'm embarking on a job hunt, but I also feel I'm due more cheddar, as I've continued to grow revenue and take on more responsibilities despite this short-term failed attempt at professional growth.

I had my performance review and didn't bring it up. (I know. I know.) My boss praised me on speaking less during meetings and said that I need to keep being patient if I want to see any growth. But, the problem is, I am being patient and if I wait for him to initiate anything, I'll be screwed. If I ask for a timeline or a list of things I can do to prove myself, it's met with defensive pushback and anger.

How do I bring this up without reviving old hostilities while genuinely expressing my desire to grow? Or is this a case of leaning in by way of getting the fuck out?

Sincerely,
FemiFrustrated

Dear FemiFrustrated,

You've come to the right place. Sami even majored in industrial and labor relations and has taken not one but TWO employment law classes. We're basically labor

experts. You should speak to an employment lawyer about this issue because it sounds like there could be legitimate discrimination at hand. According to what we've read, there are two ways you can prove it; you can either prove that the company on a whole discriminates against women, or you can try to prove that in your situation you were discriminated against. According to what you're saying, it seems like you might even have documentation about it that you can show to a lawyer. It may cost some money but could be worth it in the end. If that seems like too big of a step for you, or if you don't have the funds to seek legal help, look at your network and see if you happen to know anyone who can provide you with advice or point you in the right direction.

Since you already got your master's degree, it may not be that bad for you to do this now. You could potentially leave the company now that you have a higher degree and could get a great job elsewhere. Also, if you win your employment lawsuit you may never have to work again! Talk about the ultimate raise.

Betches

2.
PLEASE ADVISE

WTF Should I Even Be Doing
with My Life?

Careers are really weird. It's like this thing that everyone does every day that defines who they are, whether that's just on paper or in a very deep way. An office is somewhere that you spend forty-plus hours a week, and you don't even get to choose the people you spend that time with. (Unless you're us and you're lucky as shit.) It's seriously a fact that you spend more time with your coworkers than with anyone else in your life. It's literally your job to be locked in a room with them all day.

And yet, despite all this, most people join the workforce after college without any kind of real understanding of how important their career choices are, or even what they want or should be doing in the first place. Of course, some people can't afford the luxury of career choice, but for the people who can, a really large number of us choose to go to a window-less white box where they mindlessly input data into an Excel spreadsheet that no one will ever look at.

So, what's the point of working? If you're committing eight to ten of your sixteen waking hours five days a week to doing shit that doesn't bring you any amount of happiness, why even do it?

To make money. Fucking duh.

So why not figure out a way to make money while doing something that you sort of like? First, a few not-so-obvious facts that most people tend to forget:

- It's very rare that a person makes a lot of money doing what they absolutely love.
- You can't succeed in doing what you like or love without making any sacrifices—at least in the beginning—i.e., your salary, location, title, industry, etc.
- No one is ever doing what they love 100 percent of the time. Maybe a little more than half your time spent in a dream job is unavoidable hard work that fucking sucks and makes you wonder why you're not just inputting data into that Excel spreadsheet that no one's reading.

- Once you start doing something you love as a job, you will probably stop loving it as much.
- Doing what you love doesn't mean choosing your favorite hobby or pastime as your career. Just because you love movies doesn't mean you should move to Hollywood tomorrow.

Normally we're not cheesy people, but when the topic is like, introspection, we have to be a little earnest. You've been warned.

To start, how about we change the phrase from "do what you love" to "love what you do." Because that's actually the goal. If we all did what we love, we would be watching Netflix for countless hours and ordering in lo mein takeout, which would result in us being literally homeless and three hundred pounds in less than a year. Sounds amazing, right? Kind of yes, kind of no.

To be completely honest, when we started Betches, our time was filled with a lot more indulgence than with work. It wasn't until we started taking the business side of things seriously that we started doing more tasks we didn't enjoy and— not coincidentally—also started finding true financial success (not to mention moving out of our parents' houses). Here's the secret: pure, endless indulgence brings neither success nor lasting happiness. In truth, human beings feel much more rewarded in the long term when we have a balance of pleasure (Netflix and lo mein) and pain (work), because we need to experience pain in contrast with pleasure in order for pleasure to *actually* be pleasurable. If everything was just amazing all the time, it wouldn't feel good anymore, because we would get used to it. Now that we have the privilege of suffering through finance meetings and difficult conversations with our employees, our pleasure comes in the form of creating new projects for our company that we feel passionately about, reaching goals we set for ourselves, and, in our case, getting to laugh at one another while recording podcasts together.

To *love what you do* on the other hand implies that you are the one in control of how you feel about your career, both the good and the bad. Having a career, by nature, is going to involve a lot of shit you don't want to do. The way to get a career that you "love" (sometimes) is to try to do something that you genuinely enjoy at least *some* piece of. That's how you make the unpleasant aspects rewarding in the long run. So, do you love arguing with people about topics that almost always have an answer if you google them, but you argue about them anyway because you love being right? Maybe try to be a lawyer. Do you love kissing people's asses in service of getting them to give you money? Get into sales. Sure, you're going to have to deal with a lot of bullshit, but you get to savor

> *Late night, come home.*
> *Work sucks, I know.*
>
> —Blink 182,
> "All the Small Things"

that amazing feeling when you close a huge deal or reach your sales goal. Are you great at convincing people upon first impression that you're a normal person when in actuality you're just great at hiding your sociopathic tendencies? Maybe try acting, reality TV, or sales. Do you love fooling people into thinking that a caviar sheet mask will help them look like Gwyneth Paltrow? Get into marketing.*

Most people think, *If only I did something I loved, then everything else would just fall into place and my life would be easy.* Actually, no, the Excel-spreadsheet direction is the easiest. The less you care, the less effort you have to put in, and the less painful it will be when you fail. But that also means there will be less of a reward when you're old as shit and looking back at your life's accomplishments, like we've seen old people do in the movies.

DO YOU KNOW YOURSELF?

Of course, you can't possibly know what you love to do without trying out a few different things first. Just like dating, it's incredibly rare that a person just knows. Did you marry your high school sweetheart? Okay, if you said yes, then fine. Whatever. This example is clearly for everyone else who's made out with

---

* It's not exactly that simple, but you get the idea.

more than one person in their whole life. The way we learn about who we want to be with long-term is by examining what went wrong in past relationships. And the way we learn how we should be making a living is a similar process of trial and error.

This means that you're never going to get it right from the get-go. So take a Xanax and chill the fuck out. You don't have to be a doctor or a lawyer or a teacher just because that's what you drew on your first-grade "When I Grow Up" worksheet. No one tells you at five that the cost of being a firefighter involves more than having to wear a fugly red hat.

On the other hand, if you're at your third company in three years and haven't learned a thing about yourself, then you should actually give me back my Xanax. To use the dating analogy, if your first two boyfriends were terrible and the relationships ended badly, and you literally keep going for the same exact type of person, it's time to see a therapist. Same with a job: if you worked at two or three companies where you've gotten fired or let go and you've made no effort to change what you're doing or reflect on why jobs keep ending badly, it's time to reevaluate. Either it's all your bosses' faults, even though they never met each other, or you need to seriously think about coming to work on time. Maybe you're in the wrong field. Or you're a crazy person. Either way, spend some time thinking about it.

We were once interviewing someone who wanted to make a change in her general career path, and we asked why. Her response was that she didn't see herself in her boss's job, which we thought was a really good barometer to know if you're on the right path. If the thought of having your boss's job doesn't appeal to you, it's probably a good idea to go in a different direction.

We'll use a less intense, more realistic example. Say you weren't fired, but you just quit a job you weren't passionate about and took the next job you weren't passionate about that paid a bit more. You were still performing the same exact duties, and your responsibilities were exactly the same, which is basically the career equivalent of continuously dating the wrong guy. Why keep making the same mistakes over and over for just a little more money and zero more happiness?

That's not to say that every move in your career must be a vertical one (that's where you move up in titles), but every new position you take should help you either weed out the kind of shit you definitely do *not* want to do, or, if you're lucky, help you identify at least one aspect of the job that you definitely *do* want to do. Like, let's say you got into sales because you thought you could make some quick money but totally sucked at it, but you happened to also realize that you just *love* making pitch decks. Maybe in your next job you take an equal type of job in terms of pay and position (a horizontal move) but the role isn't in sales; it's in marketing or design. Maybe take a design class to see if that's what's calling you, and to make yourself more marketable the next time you apply for a job. Then one day a happier, more-fulfilled you can be like: "And you get a pitch deck, and *you* get a pitch deck!"

Those are called *carefully considered career moves.* Consider that shit carefully! You want to be a grandma and feel proud of what you've learned. Which includes both the multitude of things you hate and the few little things that you love. And like, hopefully you saved money for your retirement along the way so you're living in the really chic old-people home instead of your resentful daughter's guest bedroom.

The more you know about yourself, the bigger the shot you have at a really fulfilling career. It's never going to be like, *Eureka! I've solved my fucking career puzzle.* Because guess what, you may change over time, industries will change, and you'll hopefully gain some skills that give you the power to do new things you once weren't able to do, or new jobs that didn't previously exist. Long story short, you're in for a long-ass, never-ending game of self-reflection, acceptance, and a lot of bitching. But at least you won't be an Excel drone (unless that's what you're into, nerd).

DO YOU ACTUALLY WANT TO BE "SUCCESSFUL"?

Based on all the career and success books that are out there, your immediate response is most likely "yes." Like *Fuck yeah, I wanna be a CEO. Fuck yeah, I wanna be successful as fuckkkk.*

But if you think about it: CEOs rarely get to do the actual things they love doing. They make a lot of high-level decisions, and they probably really loved doing whatever they were doing right up until the point when they became CEOs. Now they just oversee other people doing what they loved. And yeah, it's great for them, they are highly successful and their paychecks reflect that, but in reality, the CEO life isn't for everyone.

The goal is to be real with yourself about what you want to spend most of your time doing, and if that thing is not being a CEO, that doesn't make you a failure.

You can still be successful without having a high-level position. We think that being successful means that you genuinely value the time you spend at work. It doesn't necessarily have to be measured by the number of digits in your salary. There are plenty of people who get paid a lot who hate their jobs. If you truly feel #blessed for the opportunity to do what you do, then you'll feel successful. Maybe you won't be written up in *Forbes* like we have (#blessed), but like, who gives a shit?

But what if your immediate response to the question "Do you care about being successful?" was actually "Not really . . ."?

Knowing yourself can also mean understanding if being a successful career person is even for you. You're not going to personally set feminism back if you truly just don't care about climbing to the top of your career ladder. TBH, if you don't really want it, you're probably not going to be the one to get there anyway. If raising children and tending to your home is what you would rather be doing and your family can afford it, then by no means should you ignore that instinct. Or if you wish to pursue an alternative that isn't raising kids, like maybe you just want great work-life balance and the opportunity to make the world a better place, go for it. I mean, that shit sounds pretty nice, too.

Of course, there's the middle ground and that's where most of us land. You'll neither be a CEO nor a stay-at-home mom, but you're content with your job and the amount of time it affords you to spend with your kids. Again, that's fine, too. Which is the point exactly. You do you, and don't let society tell you who that is.

> *Charlotte: The women's movement is supposed to be about choice and if I choose to quit my job, that is my choice.*
>
> *Miranda: The women's movement? Jesus Christ, I haven't even had coffee yet.*
>
> —Sex and the City

It's important to remember that people are constantly changing. One day you might not want to join the workforce, and you may decide to stay home, take care of your children, and bake brownies. Then the next day you realize, wow, those brownies you make are literally the shit and everyone asked for the recipe. Maybe you want to sell them? Maybe everything you make is so good that you want to start a cooking blog? Or maybe that sounds like a nice idea, but it's really not for you. Success looks different for everyone, and once you define and accept what it looks like for you everything becomes a bit clearer. As DHT once said, listen to your heart.

Inspirational *Bridesmaids* Scene About Ever-Evolving Personalities

Helen: It's funny how people change, isn't it?

Annie: Yeah, I mean, I don't know. Do people really change?

Helen: I think they do.

Annie: Yeah, but I mean, they still stay who they are, pretty much.

Helen: I think we change all the time.

Annie: I think we stay the same, but grow I guess a little bit.

Helen: I think if you're growing, then you're changing.

Annie: But I mean, we're changing from who we are, which we always stay as.

Helen: Not really, I don't think so.

Annie: I think so.

Helen: I don't.

SHIT YOUR GUIDANCE COUNSELOR
SHOULD HAVE TOLD YOU

As postgrad betches, we fondly recall living the easy life in college. Our days were spent smoking weed and ordering Jimmy John's, and our nights were spent blacking out and wearing heels that we can't even imagine walking a block in now.

Much like our metabolisms at twenty-one, a lot has changed since we got our diplomas. And in that time, we've realized a lot (thanks, Kylie) about what we should've been focusing on in school versus what we actually focused on.

A lot of college kids make the mistake of majoring in something that they think will make them a lot of money. All those internet articles about how sociology majors can't find jobs spark mental images of moving into a parent's basement and scare many people into getting on a finance track. They take their parents' pressure on them to be really successful, combine that with a lack of any clue what they're really good at and passionate about, and wind up trying to work toward a career that they don't really give a shit about. Think about it: lots of people pick their college major during their senior year of high school, while they're still living in their parents' houses and have had no significant chance of exposure to anything besides the perspectives of these two random adults and maybe a few siblings. The chances that at eighteen years old your perspective has an exact correlation to what you as an individual will want for your future self are very slim. It's literally not possible to have a realistic view of what you want, because you simply don't have the experience or any idea of the scope of possibilities that are out there. So you end up picking what seems financially lucrative, or what you took on as your high school "identity" based on what classes or clubs you were most successful in.

While this temporarily placates Mom and Dad and makes them feel secure, it actually sets you back because you think you have it all figured out, but you haven't even seen what your real options are. If you step onto your college campus with your mind fully made up that you're going to become X, you're going to be behind when you enter the real world and realize you've wasted years pursuing X when you don't actually want X. Now you have to spend even more time coming to that realization, and then going through the pain of deciding that what you thought you wanted isn't actually what's best for you, and then go through the excruciating transition to something else entirely. That's at least two years of your life right there. However, you can spare yourself from at least two years of pain if you approach college (and life in general) with an open mind toward what you might want. Try listening to yourself and not your parents, for once. We honestly don't know anyone whose parents were *that* angry that their kid tried to pursue an alternate career path, other than the mom from *Center Stage* ("It's *your* dream, Mom!").

Even better, begin this mindset before you get to college. In truth, our guidance counselors should have spent less time telling us what we needed to get on our SATs to get into a college with a good football team and more time on actually, you know, guiding us. Guidance counselors should have told you that you shouldn't follow the money but instead, if you follow your skills, the money is more likely to follow. They should have shown you that there's a future *after* college. College itself isn't the whole point. Hopefully, this book can be like a little paper version of a guidance counselor. But if you're already spending sleepless nights at your Goldman Sachs desk and wondering where it all went wrong, we're very sorry we couldn't get to you sooner. When you're finished reading, give it to your little sister.

This doesn't mean we're suggesting you get a job where you're going to be a penniless sitar player (although that sounds like a sick hobby). You'll always have the opportunity to make money as long as you're good at what you do, know how to promote yourself, and there's at least some demand for your skills. So instead of thinking about what job you want to have, think about what skills and interests you already have for which there is at least some demand, and work on cultivating a network of people who can help you gain success there.

We're going to give you a little rundown of our own career-path fuckups, because, hopefully, they'll inspire you to learn from our mistakes.

Aleen majored in biology and wanted to follow in her mother's footsteps to become a doctor. She spent four years of college working ridiculously hard in premed classes and fly-counting labs, summers interning in medical labs, and working her ass off in pursuit of a medical career. When we started Betches, Aleen was still planning to take the MCAT. But even before we started it, she knew that she needed to take a year off because twenty-two felt a little too early in life to be burned out on a career she *hadn't even started yet*. Luckily, we started Betches right then, so that year off was worthwhile in the end. But the realization of the impending burnout was actually pretty important because Aleen realized that while she was "good at science," she was only really interested in that career path because being a doctor meant "being success-ful" to her. Once she paused she quickly realized—and so did her parents—that there are many other ways of succeeding in your career. So instead of sticking to the prescribed plan, she followed her instinct that there was something about Betches that felt right, and was able to hone her creativity and humor, which she was actually way better at than understanding cellular and molecular biology. Ugh.

Sami grew up assuming that she was going to be a lawyer for three reasons: lawyers make a lot of money, she was relentlessly argumentative as a child, and, also, Elle Woods. Cut to LSAT class during the summer after sophomore year, where she could barely sit through a single class without being bored to tears and leaving halfway through. When she really thought about what it meant to be a lawyer, she realized it was not going to be nearly as *glamorous* as she had assumed, and also that most legal quandaries aren't going to be solved by knowing the rules of perm maintenance. (Yes, she seriously thought that being a lawyer was going to be glamorous and not like, ten years of thankless drudgery.) So she said goodbye to the LSAT and never looked back, then started looking into HR jobs because it was part of her major and seemed interesting. She got an internship working in talent development at a large insurance company the summer after junior year and ended up really enjoying working with people. She now takes the lead on all issues concerning HR and our organizational structure.

Jordana had zero clue what she wanted to do with her life, but she did know she didn't want to be poor. So instead of thinking about the life she wanted, she just applied for a bunch of different jobs, including many in the fashion industry that seemed like they had a decent salary. But Jordana is ensembly challenged. Spending her entire childhood wearing the hand-me-downs of her five sisters gave her the fashion sense of Mugatu. Somehow, cue the hysterical laughter of our friends, she applied and got an interview for a job as an American Eagle buyer. But during the interview, when she was asked about all the latest fashion trends, she panicked and just blurted out one random phrase: *horizontal stripes*. Clearly, she didn't get the job. The lesson here is pretty simple. When you try to change yourself to fit a job because either you think you'll make a lot of money or you'll just take whatever interview you can get, it never works. You won't be passionate about it, and it winds up being a waste of your time.

You need to live for yourself. Your parents, your friends, and your professors may have dreams for you and how your life will turn out, but at the end of the day you're the only one who has to actually live it. College is a time for fucking around, but the more politically correct term for doing that is *exploring*. So if you're lucky enough to still be in college, spend some time remembering what you loved doing and got excited about as a kid and dip your foot into a bunch of different professions. Would you rather take the road less traveled and make less money but be truly passionate and excited about life, or would you rather be a lawyer? Yeah, that's what we thought.

WHAT IF YOU STILL JUST DON'T KNOW?

If you're like, *WTF, this didn't help me at all!* Ummm, sorry? We never claimed that this book is like the end-all guide to figuring out your shit. We obviously don't know your life. But honestly, there are only a few people who can say with 100 percent confidence that what they're doing is what they should be doing and the rest are full of shit. So, do you and don't stress about it.

The best you can do is gather data. Gather data on your thoughts and feelings. Yes, this sounds cheesier than a quesadilla, but it's true. Just like every time you fuck up it's a learning experience, every job you have—good, bad, or ugly—gives you information that you can analyze and make some conclusion about what you like to do, hate to do, could stand to do, would rather shoot yourself in the foot than do again, and what you're actually really good at.

The worst thing you can do is nothing. If you know you need to make a change in your career but are too afraid to rip off the Band-Aid, so instead just keep sitting in your uncomfortable chair at your pointless job day after day, counting the hours until you can bounce, then you might as well just forget about everything, including your like, hopes and dreams. Every day that you put off making the change you need is one less day you have to pursue your actual passion and goal.

We know—who needs Tony Robbins when you have us?

What Your Job Says About You

PR: You want a fun job but don't care about making that much money. You also love that you're in PR and love the idea of working with major brands and celebrities. Your job (and everything else you do) is "OMG, so fun." Your fave type of outfit to wear to work is cute high-waisted jeans, a white tee, and your leather jacket draped over your shoulders because you're like, always cold. When your coworker asks what you want to get for lunch.you almost always answer, "Ugh, somewhere healthy *pleaseeee*." You spend a lot of time on dating apps on the weekends, and there has yet to be a mimosa cheers that you didn't boomerang.

Accountant/lawyer/consultant: You're pretty smart and care about making money but don't know WTF to do with your life.

Doctor: You say you just want to help people, but if someone took away the potential of making $300K, then you might change your mind. Any hospital you work at is always considered *your* hospital. Even if you just started working there yesterday. You feel like you're smarter than everyone else and, let's face it, you probably are. Spending ten years making no money and learning all day will take its toll in that way. Your love life is in shambles because you never have time to date since you spend most of your time at the hospital. You think your attending is really hot, but he's married.

Teacher: You plan to marry rich. Summers off are ah-mazing.

HR: Your name is Susan. Your Instagram bio reads, "Plant Mom." You bring lunch every day and it's usually leftover roasted chicken and brussels sprouts or broccoli. You get really excited when the nail place you go to is playing HGTV in the background. Unlike everyone at work, your cat truly loves you.

Influencer/blogger: You think you've made it the first time you post a discount code with your name in front of it, even if it's for laxative tea. If you haven't already seen a therapist, you probably should. You have a tendency to close Instagram and then reopen it literally a second later. You love that you get to wake up whenever you want. You hate when people comment and don't like. If you didn't post your feet walking up the StairMaster, a super-chic pose on the Pilates reformer, or how many miles you did on the elliptical, did you even work out?

Finance: You looooooove money and could pinpoint the street value of Adderall at any moment of the day. The guys in finance are hot, rich, and have no souls, but hey, you don't, either. Birds of a feather . . .

Real estate/sales: You watched one episode of *Million Dollar Listing* and were like, *kk that's going to be me.* You also loooooove money but are less into school and long hours than the finance girl. You love posting pictures of your "properties." You hate that you don't live in any of them.

Freelancer: You don't remember the last time you put on real pants, as you are slowly becoming one with your pajamas. Seamless/Grubhub/whatever you use to order food often sends you discounts on your third order of the day. The barista at the Starbucks across the street from your apartment thinks you're a mole person since you wear ill-fitting sweatpants 70 percent of the time, but then you go back to the couch and turn on your TV and feel totally okay with that.

Advertising/media: You couldn't figure out what you wanted to do but the thought of law school or taking out loans for additional schooling made you more nauseated than the smell of warm jungle juice the morning after a pregame. You hated school and tests but love having fun and feeling like you're in charge of shit. You switch off between loving and hating your job every other day but you're also convinced that your job is the most important job in the world because, as you told everyone in a drunk rant last night, advertising like, runs this country's economy.

Engineer/tech nerd: You're a genius, you can just stop reading this book now.

BREAKDOWN OF INDUSTRIES AND ENVIRONMENTS

Now, if none of that was helpful because you still can't identify yourself with a certain job, well then, maybe we can help break down different industries; after all, job environment plays a huge factor in whether it would be a good fit. Say you're really good at beauty tutorials but you wouldn't ever want to work in a big gray-carpeted corporate office, then maybe the right route for you is freelance makeup artist. On the other hand, say you need deadlines to work, love brainstorming, and seriously care what people comment on each other's instagrams, well then, maybe you should be in media. Let's discuss popular industries and what it's like to work in them.

Fashion/PR: Exactly as *The Devil Wears Prada* led you to believe this job would be. Even though fashion is starting to be a little more accepting of sizes above subzero, people are still quite focused on appearance. They praise Ashley Graham on Instagram but talk shit about her thighs behind her back. This industry is harsh, self-important, and doesn't really pay that much. Why are people in it? Because they care about seeming cool, or maybe because they actually give a shit what Pantone's color of the year is.

Tech: If we learned anything from *Silicon Valley*, it's that this world is changing faster than your tampon on a heavy-flow day. This can be highly stressful, but if you're a really skilled developer, coder, or engineer, then this is fine for you. If you're not that good, you'll know right away because you won't get work or you'll get eaten alive. If you're a female techie, now's the time to swing for the fences, as tech companies are needing to even out their ratios ~~for press purposes~~, because they believe in diversity and being socially conscious, *of course.*

Media/advertising: If you're personable, outgoing, and looking for a bullshit job where you get to do very little but have the opportunity to be paid more down the road, find a media job in a large corporate company. All media companies are competing with one another, so they're all spending a shit ton of money on pointless employee perks like beer on tap, expensive beverages that claim to be healthier than water, and the ability to work on a couch in a different room from your desk. Gasp.

Entertainment: You have to do an incredible amount of bitch work, ass-kissing, and sliding into people's DMs to move up in this industry. Like, if you even want to write on a show, the amount of coffee you need to retrieve in your career will surpass the amount of alcohol you drank in college. If you really want to be the next Ava DuVernay, though, know that it's going to be a lot of rejection and disappointment, but it is possible to get there, so keep going.

Career student: Rewarding AF. Not financially, though. And the only time that philosophy degree will help you is when you're discussing *Game of Thrones* fan theories.

Medicine/law: Even though the two are different, we grouped them together because they're similar in that you have to put in a lot of work and hours—and also money—with very little sleep or salary to make a lot of money at some point very far in the future. Plus, you have to be really into reading to succeed in either field.

Finance: You'll have to deal with a lot of bros and douchebags to be in this industry. Everyone talks really fast and assumes

WTF Should I Do for a Job?

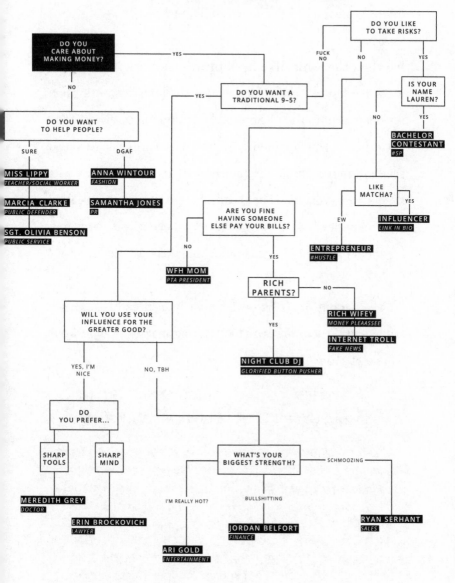

you know what they're talking about when they use terms like *EBIDTA* and *vested equity*. Couldn't care less about changing interest rates? Then don't go into finance.

All the other shit, like agriculture: Honestly, this industry is the hardest to write about because we know very little about it. Aleen went to the College of Agriculture and Life Sciences at Cornell, yet still, not much info from us. Farmers have one of the most important jobs in the country, and do you know what they have to rely on? The weather. That's right, the weather. And then they have to deal with these huge corporations forcing them to accept buy-outs or kicking them off their land.

Yes, we left out a lot of different industries because, you know what, there are way too fucking many, and you know what else? You'll get over it.

Inspirational Career Betch: Mindy Kaling

Work hard, know your shit, show your shit, and then feel entitled. Listen to no one except the two smartest and kindest adults you know, and that doesn't always mean your parents. If you do that, you will be fine.
—Mindy Kaling, *Why Not Me?*

In her book *Is Everyone Hanging Out Without Me? (And Other Concerns)*, Mindy Kaling documents her life and childhood and how she got to be where she is today.

The daughter of immigrant parents employed as a doctor and an architect, Mindy could've very simply chosen the suggested path of following in those footsteps. Instead, she made her own way with pretty much no family connections. And she gave herself her own time to explore what she liked before she settled on a career path. She got into Dartmouth, joined a sorority, hated it and dropped out, and spent her summers interning for Conan O'Brien and exploring her love of comedy. Like most of us, Mindy had to have a few shitty internships before she could figure out what the fuck she wanted to do with her life. She described her time as a production assistant on John Edward's *Crossing Over* as "depressing" and one of the worst job experiences she's ever had. Mindy channeled her skills so well that she became the only female writer of *The Office* at twenty-four and starred as our favorite character Kelly Kapoor. She did such an amazing job on that show that she later got her own show, *The Mindy Project*, and has written two books. She had a baby on her own and mastered the art of being ridiculously successful while not taking herself too seriously. Mindy proves that it's still possible to succeed no matter your background or what your parents do, even if you don't have all the built-in advantages of being a white, straight man in Hollywood. If you work your ass off, figure out what you're really good at, and advocate for yourself, success can follow.

TL;DR

If you're lucky enough to have the opportunity of choosing what you want to do in life, make sure not to take it for granted. Do some soul-searching but don't take too long. The most important thing is to identify something that you might like to do and then do it. The rest will follow because even if you hate it, you learned something.

And if you totally forgot everything you just read because you smoked before starting the chapter, here's what you missed:

- If you only aim to do what you love, you (a) might not make money doing it, or (b) might end up hating it.
- Make sure you take something away from each job you leave—no, we don't mean a company stapler—i.e., take every opportunity to learn about yourself.
- Don't pressure yourself to do something you don't want to do. It's okay to not aspire to be a CEO if that's not want you want for yourself.
- Your guidance counselor probably sucked. Just saying.
- Then we gave you a bunch of guides to help you narrow down your career because we're amazing.

While you're soul-searching, remember that work doesn't define you, even though it's what you spend most of your time doing. Instead, what you do should complement your personality, passion, and skill set. Remember, it's not about figuring out how to do what you love but how to love what you do.

Dear Betches,

I need some help from you Betches. I currently work at an ad agency in NYC and absolutely love my job; I had my own business before (small ad agency), and I loved it, too! However, sometimes I feel that it's not my PASSION. Which at times makes me feel lost and confused. Ultimately, I do not want to work for someone else and want to start something of my own. I am twenty-three years old, and I know I have so much time to figure out what I want to do with my life. But how do you go about finding what you truly love to do? Side note: my personality is very nonchalant about a lot of things. So I'm not sure if I actually will ever be *super* passionate about something because that's just how I am.

Do you have any guidance tips for figuring out what the eff you want to do with your life/for a living?

Ugh, sincerely,
Life-Loving-but-Kind-of-Lost Betch

Dear Loving Life,

First of all, congratulations to you on having already owned your own business before twenty-three. Many people don't even start doing their own laundry before that age. It seems clear that you're ambitious and are

willing to work hard at whatever you're doing. Figuring out what you're passionate about can be really hard, especially if you're good at something you're already employed at and it seems daunting to start over.

The best way to find out what will make you truly happy is to start by thinking critically about what you want and why you want it. A lot of the time we assume that we want to do things just because we've already put a lot of effort into going down a specific path. We wrongly accept that we need to make a certain amount of money to be happy, that we don't have anything unique to offer in other fields, or that we'll fail at trying something different. This makes us complacent or too afraid to find the thing that will actually make us happy to focus on. Think about what parts of your job you'd do less of in a perfect world. A lot of the time, you can use this understanding to reshape your current position in your job instead of leaving it entirely so that you're more passionate about everything you're working on.

It's really difficult to evaluate your own life, since you're in it and can be held back by previously held false beliefs about yourself. Maybe you want to see a psychologist or a life coach, or anyone you trust who has no skin in the game regarding your career to see if they can help you figure out what you actually enjoy doing. Hopefully this person can mentor and advise you about what the right career shift would look like for you and help you map out steps you'd need to take to get there.

Figure out who you are and what you want by asking

yourself some questions and answering them truthfully. When you're empowered with the right mentor and the right sense of yourself, you can start shaping your career into one that works for you. Ask yourself what you can offer and do that's significantly different from what the best people in the field you love do, and what talents, abilities, and skills make you stand out.

Finally, use all this information to connect the dots in your life. You've already mentioned that you're more chill and not necessarily a super passionate person, but maybe that's just because you haven't encountered something you're super passionate about yet. Or maybe you're right and you're just not that enthusiastic of a person. Only you can really know, but for fuck's sake don't lie to yourself.

Work sucks when you spend all day counting down the minutes until you can leave for happy hour. Only once you look at your life truthfully and objectively can you figure out the best place to channel your creative energy and hard work.

Good luck!
Betches

3.
TO WHOM IT MAY CONCERN

How to Get a Job

So now that you've figured out the types of jobs that fit your passions and skill set, it's time to get started actually finding one.

Women are often taught to be quiet and to let men do the pursuing. From a young age, femininity is associated with being timid, modest, and choosing between the many men who will chase you. I mean, the entire theory behind *The Rules* is about *not* putting yourself out there in order to succeed in your relationships. Unfortunately for the workingwoman, career success largely hinges on doing the opposite. If we accept the rules that have been so aggressively hammered down our throats about how women are supposed to act and apply them to the working world, we'll be doomed to a life where we merely take what's handed to us instead of choosing our own destinies. The next sections will give you tips about how to overcome this way of thinking, go after what you want, and advocate for yourself. You're welcome.

The job search is your first opportunity to practice being aggressive with your career moves. Much like dating, before you look for a job you should know what you want, make sure you have your shit together, and then prepare to keep trying despite a ton of rejection. You should also be prepared to do a lot of the rejecting yourself. You wouldn't marry the first guy who gave you any attention, would you? Exactly. So don't take a job without seeing what's out there. For more on dating, check out our amazing book *I Had a Nice Time and Other Lies . . . How to Find Love & Sh*t Like That.*

Remember: it's okay to apply for jobs where you don't necessarily qualify for *all* the criteria on the job advertisement. Statistically, men are much more likely to apply for jobs where they meet only 60 percent of the qualifications. Meanwhile, women only apply for jobs where they meet 100 percent of the criteria. Looking at the data, the logical conclusion is that men assume that they can figure it out along the way, whereas women are less sure of themselves.

So while you shouldn't go around applying for jobs that

require ten years of real-world experience the day you graduate college, if you have confidence in your ability to succeed at a position but you're only semi-proficient in Microsoft Excel rather than an expert, apply anyway. You can always like, take a class; it's not that hard. You may be afraid that it's a waste of your time to apply for jobs you're not completely qualified for, but an interviewer could see a certain intrinsic quality in you that they love and realize they want to prioritize more. Job descriptions, much like dating-app profiles, rarely give the full picture. Also, even if you don't get the job, every application and interview is a learning experience and a chance for you to get important feedback. Plus, you could meet someone who, while they might not hire you for this particular job, could help you in a different situation or with a different role.

THE IMPORTANCE OF FAKING IT

Unlike orgasms, it's not a terrible idea to exaggerate a little about your skill set. We live in the Information Age: it's called fucking Google and it helps you learn how to do things that you don't already know but you might be asked to do once you're actually hired for a job. Literally everyone, from entry-level positions to CEOs, are googling how to do stuff like find the average of numbers in Excel, so don't think of it as cheating to say you're a little more proficient at something than you are. Think of it as a "learning opportunity."

Another important thing to note is that you should focus on applying to jobs that you actually want. Despite popular opinion, it's better to apply to five jobs that are a great potential fit and you could be really passionate about than to ten jobs that are just like, whatever. Applying to fewer, better jobs is not only a well-suited use of your time but it'll ensure that you're putting more effort into the applications themselves. Don't send out ten identical cover letters and expect that anyone's going to be fooled into thinking you give a shit about an opportunity. Just like you shouldn't accept every date with a douchey loser who asks for your number, don't apply for every job that comes up from a basic search on Monster.com. Your time is precious, and the more time you spend on things you don't actually care about, the less time you have for the things you do.

> Whenever you are asked if you can do a job, tell 'em, "Certainly I can!" Then get busy and find out how to do it.
> —Theodore Roosevelt

BUILDING A RÉSUMÉ

First things first. It's time to make a résumé. Think of a résumé like an online-dating profile, only employers give less of a shit about your height and bikini shots and care more about your college degree and work experience. A résumé is a time to do something betches do best: brag about themselves. It might feel weird and kind of boastful to write out a list of your top accomplishments, but this is not the time to be modest about your achievements. Employers have no way of knowing how selective that scholarship program you made it into was or how you were ranked top saleswoman five quarters in a row unless you tell them that shit on your résumé. Much like when your boyfriend fucked up when he got your salad dressing mixed in instead of on the side, they're not mind readers. A résumé is a time to tell employers all the reasons they would be idiots not to hire you by highlighting what you do best.

Here's a fun fact: the average prospective employer spends just six seconds looking at your résumé, so you'd better make sure there's something that catches their eye—in a positive way. We all know your go-to internship strategy was taking your most try-hard sorority sister's résumé and basically swapping in your info, but if you're looking for a legitimate job that's not going to crush your soul, that's no longer going to fly.

Here are some tips for making your résumé stand out so you don't wind up being passed over for promotion at a California Pizza Kitchen.

Shit to Delete from Your Résumé

Your ridiculous email address: Your middle school email may have been the envy of every basic bitch around, but ReesesPeanutButterLover89@yahoo.com is not going to make an employer take you seriously. Make your email your full name @gmail.com so the person reading your résumé doesn't have to wonder if you're using dial-up AOL from your parents' basement. Hotmail is death.

Your entire street address: No one is sending you fucking letters. Shorten it by only including the city and state to make room for more important info, like your fake proficiency in Spanish.

Spelling and grammar mistakes: Nothing makes you look like you don't give a shit more than a spelling or grammar error in your résumé. Proofread. Seriously, proofread. We can't tell you how many times we've rejected candidates right off the bat for using the wrong form of *to*. It's that easy to eliminate a candidate, and how better to reduce the pool of annoying interviews we'll potentially have to conduct than to immediately cut the people who didn't even take the time to check their grammar. This isn't a take-home essay for some bullshit elective you're taking. This is your career. Don't be lazy. Send it to your mom to proofread if you need to. She'll be incentivized to help because checking your résumé means she's one step closer to not paying for all your shit anymore. Plus, she knows that stuff, because public school was way stricter back in the day.

Your babysitting job from high school: If you're applying for a job as a paralegal in 2018, no one is going to care that you babysat for the Goldbergs from 2007 to 2010, no matter how amazing you were at Connect Four.* Get rid of all irrelevant work experience that doesn't directly contribute to showing an employer that you have skills in the job you're actually applying for. Unless the person you're interviewing with happened to go to the same summer camp as you, he or she is not going

---

* Certain jobs, such as an executive assistant, might actually want to see that you worked in the service industry or had a job in retail. They want to know that you are well organized and good at mundane tasks, so if you're applying for an entry-level position or one that doesn't require a ton of high-level thought, it *is* okay to write about that summer waitressing job you had, but make sure to stress that the skills you were taught were "hospitality," *not* "dealing with bitchy customers."

to think it's relevant that you were an uncertified lifeguard at Camp Lakota for two years. (But if you google the interviewer and see Camp Lakota in their Facebook interests, make that shit size-14 font.)

ADVANCED TIPS THAT WILL GET YOU A JOB AT LIKE, GOOGLE

Despite all the aforementioned rules, you shouldn't be afraid of showing who you really are with your résumé. Use the word *I*; write an objective with a little enthusiasm in it so the employer feels like they're talking to an interesting human instead of a robot set to "professional" mode.

Example of a shitty objective: To assume a position in human resources at a large company.

Example of a good objective: I have a passion for HR and making employees feel great about where they work. I would love to leverage my past experience at a smaller start-up to a company I admire for their breadth of opportunities and positive learning environment.

See how the first example makes you think this applicant does not actually believe in the objective, and the second makes you actually want to meet the person behind the statement? It's personal; it includes a mention of relevant experience and some compliments about the company she's applying to. Don't be so focused on being professional that you seem generic. That's like writing that you love "food and music" on your dating profile. Nobody cares because literally everyone likes food and music, and you will quickly be left-swiped.

Here are some tips that former Google Product Manager Jon Youshaei (who we found on Google, obvi) wrote about in his *Forbes* article, "6 Secrets of Great Resumes, Backed by Psychology," that will make your résumé stand out, and not because you forgot to remove [insert company name here] in your cover letter.

Use numbers: Don't just say you were a "top seller at *X brand* last year," use the number you sold (as long as that number is impressive) or some other number that sounds good in context. Don't just say you built your company's email subscription numbers, say that you got their email list from zero to 100,000 subscribers in a year, or give a percentage of growth. Logic, evidence, and facts are more convincing than you trying to bullshit someone into thinking you did a better job than you did. Even if all you did was launch a Facebook site for your dad's dentistry office, give the percentages of growth in engagement as long as that growth isn't zero.

Everything's a competition: If you won awards or got into a certain program, say how few people were selected, thereby showing how great of an achievement it was. Unlike your Little League participation trophy, special recognition means more when fewer people qualify for it. Example: "Selected for the National Creativity Award (ten chosen from a pool of more than ten thousand applicants)." This also helps explain why what you've accomplished is impressive in case your interviewer has no idea WTF the National Creativity Award even is. But if it's some sort of participation award, then please don't include it.

Lightly stalk someone who works there: Go to networking events and meet someone who works in the company. They can tell you what the company really wants to see on your résumé or buzzwords that get employees there more excited than you get when your dog does literally anything. They can tell you where the company is going and the type of people they're looking for, and you can use that inside information to position yourself in that way. If the company loves hearing the word *empowering*, then include it a few times on your résumé to show that you really align with the culture. Also, by ~~forcing~~ kindly requesting that this person review your résumé, you're getting your foot in the door at the company and they might even recommend you to the hiring manager. But don't be a creep about it.

Name-drop, but not in the pretentious way: People feel safer and that you're more impressive when you show that you've already worked with established institutions or brands. So if you went to Harvard, now's a good time to mention that. If you've worked with Coca-Cola or Apple, an employer will assume you're not so big of a fuckup that you can't have big-name clients. Unlike Sonja Morgan bragging about partying with JFK Jr., employers actually do want to know that you've succeeded or worked with legitimate companies.

A NOTE ON LYING ON YOUR RÉSUMÉ

Just like guys shouldn't write on their dating profiles that they're six foot three when they're actually five foot eight, you shouldn't completely make things up on your résumé. Don't pretend you held a position that you never did, and don't say you took on major responsibilities that you have literally no experience with.

In addition to the eventual potential embarrassment and qualifying as sociopathic, it'll be pretty clear in an interview when you can't speak to any personal experiences that were on your résumé, and it will be awkward when you're fired within six months of getting the job because you can't do anything you said you could.

However, just like most guys who are five foot eleven write that they're six feet tall, a little fudging on a résumé is expected and not a huge deal. So, like, if you built an email list of 73,000 and you call it 75,000, no one's going to call the cops on you (as long as the information isn't public). But if you claimed to be the CEO of your mom's ob-gyn office, chances are you're going to get caught. It's simple: exaggerate a little, not a lot.

> **Professor Callahan:** *Do you have a résumé?*
>
> **Elle:** *Yes, I do. Here it is!*
>
> **Professor Callahan:** *It's pink.*
>
> **Elle:** *Oh! And it's scented! I think it gives it a little something extra, don't you think?*
>
> —Legally Blonde

MY RÉSUMÉ IS PERFECT, WHAT NOW?

So now you have a one-page piece of art that perfectly describes who you are and where you've been. Now WTF do you do with it? Time to start looking for the perfect job. People get jobs in a lot of different ways, and each way comes with its own annoying pros and cons. Let's break them down.

Your dad!: Every betch knows the girl who doesn't know WTF to do with her life, so she just winds up working for her rich dad (or mom) who owns a business. You're not fooling anyone by pretending you've always had a passion for the family lightbulb distribution business. We're all for a family-legacy job where your cover letter is obsolete because your dad already knows you're perfect, but don't try and bullshit anyone into thinking you could have gotten the job fairly either way. Working for your family allows you to do fun shit like leave work early so you can go hang out with the boss's wife (your mom), but it's also annoying to spend all day with your family. Plus, your coworkers will probably resent you for not having to work as hard. If you need further proof, take a look at the accusations of nepotism in the casting of *Girls*. I mean, it's not your fault your dad's obsessed with you or something!

A NOTE ON NEPOTISM

Nepotism is when people with influence give jobs to their friends or family. See: Jared Kushner, all the Kardashians, or any other famous person's kid. In the business world, it's very common, so as long as it doesn't affect you directly you kind of just have to deal with it. Work hard and your boss, assuming he or she isn't delusional, will recognize that you're better than his idiot son and hopefully promote you fairly. If he doesn't, maybe consider taking your experience and skills elsewhere.

Online: Companies like Monster and Indeed have a shit ton of jobs in every field that you can apply for. Remember that you're applying with like, a million other applicants though, so make sure your résumé and cover letter stand out. Also, if you absolutely love a certain company and think you'd kill it working there, check out their website to see if they're hiring, or find the hiring manager on LinkedIn. Then work really, really hard on your application so that they understand that not only are you qualified but it's also your dream job. But don't seem desperate, ew.

Recruiters: Recruiters are people who are hired by companies to find them the best possible candidates for a job so that the companies don't have to spend their valuable time reading résumés and screening for psychos. A recruiter will figure out your skill set and shop you around to a bunch of companies like you're a house on the market and they're a licensed Realtor. These people can be great, especially since they only get paid if you get a job, so they're incentivized to negotiate on your behalf and help you navigate the interview process.

Networking: Networking is like a socially acceptable version of social climbing, and a lot of it involves being fake as shit in order to make a connection with anyone who could possibly help you get a job. If done right, good networking can get you anything, from a foot in the door at an interview you really want to the highest-level security clearance at the White House.

NETWORKING TO FIND A JOB

Because we're relatively antisocial and enjoy the art of never branching out, it's not surprising that we didn't find mentors or advisers for our business until several years in. Like we mentioned earlier, we even joined WeWork in an effort to meet other business owners but wound up avoiding everyone else who worked there. That said, we've learned a lot from our mistakes and now have some valuable advice to share.

Here are things to keep in mind when you're forced to socialize for the sake of your career:

Quality not quantity: Unless you're a fucking club promoter sending a mass text to 150 college girls, your connections are much more about their substance than the sheer number of them. You should make a list of around twenty people in your life who could be really helpful for job connections, specifically for the types of fields you're interested in. You know they fall into the "quality" category rather than the "quantity" one when you could realistically and nonawkwardly ask them to catch up over coffee or dinner without it being like, insanely weird. Don't, however, feel strange about using a third-party connection if it fits your situation, even if it is a bit of a stretch. Let's say your best friend's mom's best friend is the president of Hearst and you want to be a writer there. It's okay to ask your friend's mom to put you in touch with her BFF given the fact that you've been close with her daughter for years. Assuming she's forgotten about that time you and your friend were caught chugging Four Lokos in her backyard, this is an easy way to leverage an existing close friendship into an outer-circle connection.

Check in with them: Once you have a list of these people, it's time to ~~suck up~~ keep in touch with them at least two to three times a year. Whether that's responding to their Instagram story or messaging them to say what's up or getting coffee, the idea is to stay in their lives just in case an opportunity arises so you won't seem like you're using them (which you are) for their connections when the time comes.

Don't be so desperate: If you show up to a college alumni event with a big stack of business cards and a try-hard attitude, no one's going to want to fucking talk to you. The best way to network is without anyone even knowing you're doing it. So, like, be casual. Talk to people about things other than work and just be yourself (your true self probably doesn't want to talk about work that much anyway, so this should be one of the easier parts). People don't want to talk to people who are only talking to them because they want something, so chill out and help yourself to some caviar while telling the panel speaker you like, absolutely love her skirt, where did she get it?

Find a way to help them: There's this thing called "the rules of reciprocity," which basically means that people are more inclined to do shit for people who do shit for them. Make them feel like they owe you by offering help in some way, even if it's small. If you're talking to someone at an event and they mention they're moving, send them an article about the best way to pack or refer them to a great moving company. People remember people who make their lives easier, fucking duh.

Introduce people to other people: Sometimes you meet people who are cool but who can't help you. Instead of dropping them and therefore seeming like a user, connect them with someone else you know, if it makes sense. Not only will you seem like a great person who does selfless good deeds, those people will be more likely to think of you and put in the effort to connect you to someone who might be important in your pursuits. Besides, the stronger your friends' network, the stronger your network.

Gather as much info as you can: Be this through an informational interview (which is where the person isn't trying to hire you, they're just telling you about their job or the company) or an industry event, a successful networking experience isn't always about directly getting you a job. It's more about you gathering as much information as you possibly can so that you can get closer to finding a position that you both qualify for and fits your needs. An event where you don't meet anyone who can help you isn't a waste of a night. An event where the only thing you learn is that very few people can pull off a yellow blazer is.

THE COVER LETTER

So now that your résumé is no longer a disaster and you've found a job opening that you like and maybe even a person who can get you an interview there, it's time to write a cover letter (or cover email, because it's not the nineties). Think of a cover letter like a college personal statement. It's a chance to ~~bullshit your way into something~~ show the company why you belong there and that they already need you, they just don't know it yet. Now, you may be tempted to make one great cover letter and click *find and replace* to change the company name and position title for each job, but doing so is—again—a waste of your time because a prospective employer will see through this move and move on to the next applicant faster than the time you maxed out your Amex buying Kylie lip kits.

Writing a great cover letter is really mostly about (1) doing your research, and (2) giving a shit. Keep these things in mind so your letter doesn't get sent around the office with everyone laughing about the girl who wrote the wrong company's name in the first sentence.

Don't just repeat your résumé: The person reading your cover letter already has your résumé and the idea of rereading it in paragraph form is most definitely more boring to them than the time your finance-bro date spent two hours explaining how hedge funds work. Fill your cover letter with a personal anecdote, why you *genuinely* want to work there, or why an experience you had would make you a great fit for this company. Do research on them and pick one or two facts you've learned to illustrate how you'll be a great fit there. Example: *Given Betches Media's history of having three entrepreneurs who started as friends, my experience working with close female mentors on meaningful projects makes me a great fit for the collaborative, supportive environment that is valued so highly there.* A prospective employee once messengered us an unsolicited, highly designed résumé and cover letter that was peppered with *Mean Girls* quotes, in-brand language, and specific examples of what she loved about

Betches Media. Needless to say, she knew her audience and got an interview.

Keep it short: Don't go over three paragraphs (or half a page). Remember, these people read a metric shit ton of applications in addition to doing their actual work, and everyone and their mother has ADD. Anything too long won't be read and, just like you wouldn't want to read your own three-page rambling short story of why you'd be a great fashion consultant, your recruiter doesn't either. Don't waste space and someone's attention span by excessively thanking the person for taking the time to read your cover letter. That's what they're supposed to do. No one likes a kiss-ass.

Don't write "To Whom It May Concern": Just start the fucking letter. No use taking up unnecessary space with a bullshit opener. If you can, find out who will be reading your résumé and put their name on the "to" line instead. If you literally have no idea, leave it blank.

Never write this phrase: "My name is _____, and I am applying for X position." Again, that's obvious, because you're already applying for the job. If you write this sentence, your cover letter will be passed by. This isn't an essay on Shakespeare's effect on history where you're trying to hit a word count, just get to the point and get to the good shit.

Check for typos: True story: In college, Jordana applied to work for Nielsen and after submitting her application realized she spelled it Nealson at least seven times throughout her cover letter. Shockingly enough, she didn't get the job. It may feel like overkill to read over your cover letter more than three times, but it's way more annoying to put the work into writing a whole mini essay only to be dismissed from consideration for a stupid mistake before the person even reads it.

Send everything as a PDF: This goes for your résumé, too. If an employer can't open your application immediately because you have it saved in some weird Apple Pages document, they're not going to request that you resend it, they're just going to move on. And don't even get us started with Microsoft Word attachments. PDFs are pretty universal and unfuckupable, so send everything in that format so your application isn't ruled out on some annoying technicality. *But Betches, I don't have Adobe.* Use Google Docs, it's free.

How to Not Have a Fucked-up Résumé

Molly Clark

21 OAK STREET, FORT LAUDERDALE, FLORIDA 33301
TEL 555-555-5555
EMAIL penguinlovaaa333@aol.com ⟶ *get a normal gmail account weirdo.*

Profile
Passionate and enthusiastic college senior who is looking for a position in a reputable organization. Looking for a position that I can utilize all the knowledge and skills I have to benefit the organization. ⟶ *vague af. who are you even talking to?*
what does this even mean??

Experience

OFFICE INTERN, BAKER CONSULTING GROUP, SEPT. 2017 - DEC. 2017

make this bullet points. use verbs, bitch.

As an office intern at Baker Consulting Group, I learned valuable skills such as marketing, human resources, and teamwork. I worked closely with the entire staff to make sure their days were running smoothly. This included doing paperwork and running office errands.

inconsistent punctuation & shit.

SOCIAL MEDIA CHAIR, ALPHA DELTA OMICRON, JAN. 2016 - JAN 2017

For my sorority, I am responsible for posting all content to our many social media platforms - Facebook, Twitter, Instagram, Snapchat. I must represent our sorority chapters online presence to entice girls to join us while also looking good to a national organization and meeting their standards.

posting pics where your friends look hot isn't a real job.

LEGAL ASSISTANT, WILSON SLATE & CLARK, JUNE 2016 - AUG. 2016

At Wilson, Clark, & Slate, I answered phones, filed paperwork, and made copies. I learned information and then gave that information to clients. Soemtimes, I would have to draft documents and invoices at the attorneys' request. *molly, no. spell good.*

we all know this means "one".

NANNY, SEVERAL FORT LAUDERDALE FAMILIES, JULY 2015 - DEC. 2016

As a nanny, I had to work with kids and make their parents feel comfortable and safe leaving them in my care. I had to follow strict schedules for the children and also walk their dog. *riveting.*

every one knows what a nanny does...

Education
Florida Atlantic University, Boca Raton, Florida — B.A. in Business, May 2018

Skills
Communication, Multitasking, Prioritizing, Social Media, Organization, Technical Skills, Marketing, Interpersonal Skills, Dependability, Leadership, Microsoft Office, Teamwork

glad you can speak. *that's what she said.* *these are the only semi-legit qualifiable skills.* *facetune is not a technical skill.*

THE INTERVIEW

So Now You Have an Interview

Even though we don't know shit about sports, if getting a job were a baseball game, the interview would be the homestretch. Everything you've done—from networking to your cover letter to your résumé—has gotten you to this point. Now it's time to run home. Actually, let's go back to the metaphor we actually understand: dating. Think of an interview like a first date. You want to seem well put together, confident, and like you don't *need* to be there. Just like on *The Bachelor*, an interviewer can tell when you're there for the wrong reasons. Don't let your voice crack or seem extremely nervous. Remember, they should want you just as much as you want them. It's not about fooling them into hiring you, because if that's your technique, you probably won't last very long. It's about both the job being the right fit for you and you being the right fit for the company. You don't need to put out (a.k.a. suck up) just to get them to like you. Let your skills and experience speak for themselves.

Interviewing can be more stressful than a college pregame with no chasers, so here are some tips to help you not fuck it up:

Have your shit together: This is a job interview, not a SoulCycle class you were too drunk to remember to cancel.

If you're not five minutes early, you're late, so make sure you leave an absurdly cushioned amount of time to get there. No one cares about the train schedule or the traffic, so do whatever you have to do to not be late. Make sure you pick out *and try on* your outfit beforehand (we've all had a situation where we picked out an outfit in our minds that did not work in reality), especially if you've been stress-carbo-loading since the last time your mom took you interview-outfit shopping, and that your résumés are printed the night before. Don't count on Staples being open in the morning.

> Success at anything will always come down to this: focus and effort. And we control both.
>
> —The Rock

If you're scrambling to get everything together right before, you're going to miss something important or appear as frazzled as you're feeling. The last thing you want is to leave an interview realizing your shirt is on inside out because you were racing out the door. Also, make sure you practice what you're going to say before you go to the interview. Practice, in addition to helping you be confident and sound smart, will also help you be less nervous. Come up with a list of intelligent, interesting questions you want to ask before the interview so you're not sitting there staring into space when they ask if you have any. Questions like:

- How do your employees develop and learn?

- How do you evaluate performance?

- Why is this position open? Why did the previous person leave?

- What are some of the company's goals in the next one to three years, and how will my position specifically help you get there?

Cautionary Betchy Job Interview Fail, Jordana Tries to Get a Real Job

Jordana had an epic interview fail in college that we can all learn a lesson from. She applied to an electronic medical records company that was conveniently located in the same city in Wisconsin where some of our friends went to school.

The company flew her out there for the interview, and she went out with our friends to the bars the night before. One thing led to another and she got so blackout drunk that she forgot to set an alarm and woke up fifteen minutes before her interview. She raced there with the worst hangover of her life, only to discover it was a full-day interview filled with a tour of the enormous premises, three separate interviews, and two aptitude and reasoning tests.

She wound up vomiting in between interviews, fell asleep during the provided lunch, all while dodging texts from her ex-boyfriend about the drunken rage texts she had sent him the night before. Needless to say, she didn't get the job and never drank the night before an interview again.

Look your best: Don't go to a job interview looking like a meth head. Make sure you wash your hair and that your nails aren't chipping. Your outfit should be cute yet appropriate for the office dress code. That means no crop tops or five-inch stilettos, no matter how good they look. You're not trying to get fucked, you're trying to get hired.

Be confident but not cocky: Don't go into the interview shaking like you're having caffeine withdrawal or sounding like you're going to cry when someone asks you what your biggest weakness is. If you don't believe in you, no one else will. On the other hand, don't sound like some overeager bullshitter who exaggerates every accomplishment she's ever had. Act like a down-to-earth person who knows her shit and brings realistic skills to the table.

Research the company: This isn't 1990, so you don't have to go to the library to find out some basic information about the company at which you're interviewing. Go to their website, peruse their LinkedIn and Glassdoor, fucking duh. You should know exactly what their business model is and a few fun facts about their history or processes, so you can relate them to your own experience and tie them into answering the question of why you'd be a good fit there. Hiring managers will like it if you ask questions specifically relating to the position or something like the company culture. Even if you don't give a shit about the answers, ask anyway and pretend to care. Think of it like a date with a super-boring rich guy. You may not think you care, but you could be wrong. If the only question you have is "So, like, what do you guys do?" you're going to be pushed out of that office faster than a group of guys in line at a club.

Don't ask about the perks: If and when you get a job offer, you can definitely ask about how many vacation days you'll get and if there's a manicurist at the office on Fridays, but don't ask that kind of stuff during the interview, especially a first-round interview. It'll make it seem like you're only there for the paid vacation and you're not that serious about the work.

> A boss's salary isn't just about money, it is about perks. It— For example, every year I get a one-hundred-dollar gas card . . . can't put a price tag on that.
>
> —Michael Scott,
> The Office

Don't talk shit: Even though we love gossip, no one wants to hire someone who's disloyal or eager to blame their issues on their previous boss. So if they ask you why you're leaving your previous company, don't talk shit about them. Sure, you might think you're leaving because your boss is a fucking idiot, but it's better to phrase that in a way that's about your personal experience, not anyone else's impact on your performance. It's like a guy who complains about his crazy ex on a first date. That's how he'll talk about you once he considers you to be the crazy ex.

Write thank-you emails: No one ever really reads a thank-you email, but it's tacky AF not to send one. You should be emailing each person who interviewed you within twenty-four hours to thank them for their time and expertise about the company. Bonus points for including something specific about your interview that resonated with you or why you feel like you'd be a great person for the job now that you've learned more. Minus points for cc'ing your mom.

Stephanie Pratt: My final objective in life is to have a handbag line. So I really want to work here just to see... You have a lot of great designers here, and the PR that you do is really awesome.

Kelly Cutrone: So you basically want to use... my clients and their inside knowledge to ultimately leave here and go make your own handbag line.

Stephanie Pratt: [Blinks.]
—The Hills

It's okay to say . . .	It's not okay to say . . .
My dream job is to grow at a company that inspires me.	My dream job is to use the money I earn here to start my own company.
My greatest strength is being a team player.	My greatest strength is my ability to party until 5:00 a.m.
In my free time I love going to the movies and hanging out with friends.	In my free time I like blacking out and texting my exes.
My past job didn't give me freedom to grow.	My last boss was a smelly bitch.
How does your company culture affect the day-to-day here?	Are there a lot of hot guys here? I'm single!
I graduated late from college because I took a leave to work on a political campaign.	I graduated late from college because I was too high to attend class.
How does the company reward initiative?	Can I leave early to pick up my dog sometimes?

DEALING WITH REJECTION

If you prepare correctly and are truly the most capable person for the position, chances are you'll get the job. But, realistically, you will also probably get rejected from a ton of jobs. And most people who don't want to hire you just won't follow up with you or give you any sort of explanation, sort of like employment ghosting. Getting rejected just means you weren't the right fit for the job and it's usually not personal. You need to ~~kiss a lot of frogs~~ feign a lot of enthusiastic handshakes before you find the perfect job for you. Rejection sucks, but that's just life. There are plenty of roles out there you'll be a great fit for, and you should look at a job rejection as a positive. At least you didn't waste your time on a position where you weren't valued, and now you're free to explore and search for the right opportunity. Every interview is a learning experience too, so if you walk away with more experience talking to people or more practice selling yourself, then it wasn't a waste of time. Move on.

NEGOTIATING THE OFFER

When you're actually offered a job, a company will usually send you an offer letter that outlines things like your salary, your responsibilities, and other boring shit. Read it carefully. And don't be afraid to negotiate the offer or ask for clarification. One study found that among recent MBA graduates, one half of men negotiated their initial salary offer while only an eighth of women did.

Before accepting an offer, it's important to consider a bunch of stuff, not just salary and benefits. That includes understanding what exactly your responsibilities and goals are, whether there's opportunity for growth within the company, and if the offer meets most of your needs.

Let's say you've recently graduated college and are interviewing for an executive assistant job. It's important to find out if you'll be booking lunch reservations for the next five years or if there's actually an opportunity to move into a bigger role in the future after you've mastered the art of lunch reservations. Let's say you're planning to have kids soon. You should find out how the company treats mothers by finding out about their family-leave policies. Explore the implications before you commit to a position or you'll find yourself right back on the job market once you take the position and realize you don't like the answers. That would be a waste of their time and yours.

You might feel like you're in no position to ask questions or make requests when you get a job offer since you haven't even started working yet. You're wrong. The window between when you get offered the job and when you sign the offer is probably the most power you'll ever have. You haven't committed to anything yet, but they've already shown their hand by giving you the offer, and it's way more annoying for them to find someone else at this point than to give in to your reasonable negotiations. Most companies will offer you something lower than they're willing to give on the chance that you'll accept the first offer out of fear of losing it.

So how do you request a higher salary without coming off as bitchy, ungrateful, or immature? There are a few really important things to remember when negotiating and we've generously outlined them for you. Yes, we know we're amazing.

Don't make it about your personal life: Don't justify asking for more money by saying how expensive your apartment is or by telling the HR rep that your dad said that once you start working he's going to cut you off. Make it very clearly about your worth as an employee. "Can you improve your offer because I'm bringing great skills to the table?" not "Can you improve your offer because I really want to start preventive Botox?"

Look it up: Let's say, hypothetically, you're applying for a marketing director job and the offer they've given is $50,000. You look up what a marketing director is paid on average in your city and it's $55,000. You then can respond with something like, "Hi, I'm so excited for the opportunity to join the team

> *Name one thing in this world that is not negotiable.*
>
> —Walter White,
> *Breaking Bad*

at Company Y and thank you for your offer. However, given the market rate for someone with my expertise and skills and how much work I'll be putting into the position, I'd appreciate if you'd consider raising the offer to $60,000." It's important to push back with a number higher than the lowest number you'll take, as the company will likely respond with a final offer that's somewhere between those two salaries. The first offer is never the final offer, and you both wind up walking a little toward the middle.

Even if they don't improve, it's very rare that they'd rescind the offer just because you asked, and the most common response will be at least a little bit of upward movement on the offer. Most people who settle for lower salaries aren't less qualified, they just didn't ask.

Inspirational Career Betch: Judge Judy

We sit across the table, and I hand him the envelope and I say, "Don't read it now, let's have a nice dinner. Call me tomorrow. You want it, fine. Otherwise, I'll produce it myself." That's the negotiation.
—Judge Judy

Judy Sheindlin, a.k.a. Judge Judy, is America's favorite cut-the-bullshit TV judge. She doesn't care about being harsh or inappropriate, and people love her for it. Because she's smart as shit, she brings that same attitude to her salary negotiations. Her show airs 260 episodes per year in 150 countries and brought in $244.7 million in ad revenue for CBS in 2016.

Knowing how much money she brings in for the network, Judy's tactic is not to negotiate outright but to simply go to dinner with the president of CBS every three years and let him know her salary demands. Then he can take it or leave it. That tactic has worked out pretty well for her, since she is now making upward of $47 million a year. She also sold her entire show archive back to CBS for $95 million. Judy proves that the best negotiation tactic is letting your work and your history speak for itself. Prove how much you're worth to a company, and they'll realize why you should be making the salary you're demanding. No emotions, just facts. This attitude toward knowing your worth has made Judge Judy the highest-paid TV star of all time. Not bad for a seventy-six-year-old grandma of thirteen.

TL;DR

Finding a job is about effort and passion. If you lack these, no one will want to hire you. If it doesn't seem like you care that much about getting the job, it's unlikely someone will have faith that you'll give a shit once you're there. Your résumé, cover letter, and interview are the three main ways to show your passion and skill set. If you carefully perfect all these steps

> *Confidence is 10 percent hard work and 90 percent delusion.*
> —Tina Fey

and you have genuine enthusiasm for the role, you're one step closer to getting your dream job and getting paid the wage you deserve. We can't guarantee you'll love it once you're there, but by practicing the skills you learned in this chapter you'll have the tools and hopefully the confidence to master the art of a job offer and not be afraid to go after what you want.

Dear Betches,

It's awesome to see women like you who so many people follow trying to make a difference. That's just like, the rules of feminism.

Anyway, I'm a senior in college, a marketing major who's about to start interviewing for real-world jobs. What's your advice on salary negotiations for initial job offers? The thought of even making a counteroffer is terrifying to me, and I feel I'm probably not alone in that. How does one go about making a counteroffer and how much should I increase by?!

Would love any advice on the topic.

Loving everything you guys do!

Sincerely,
Timid Betch

Dear Timid Betch,

Good for you for being proactive about your job search. It's important to start early and not wait until you've graduated college to start looking for positions. Despite all the free food and laundry, we all want to minimize the amount of time spent living with our parents as much as possible.

When it comes to salary negotiations, the amount you're supposed to counteroffer totally depends on what the job and salary are. If your job gives you hourly wages, you're obviously looking at different types of numbers than if you're being paid a yearly salary. Other things to consider are if the position comes with medical and dental benefits, vacation time, the family leave policies, and 401(k) options. These kinds of things may seem unimportant now, but the more you grow into your position and your career, the more you're going to have to worry about your future and the type of company that you really want to be working for. Even though it seems really difficult and daunting, all good things are really difficult, so you just have to go for it. No one has ever died asking for a job (that we're aware of), so don't be afraid to go in there with as much confidence as you can.

A generally good rule for initial job-offer negotiations is to ask for a 10 percent increase from their first offer. We know it's really intimidating to ask for more money, but here's the secret: they are expecting you to ask for more, and they might even respect that you had the courage to ask.

You should express how much value you'll be bringing to the company when negotiating your salary and stay clear of discussing any personal finance matters that affect how much money you're requesting.

It's important to remember that there's always room for negotiation. Everyone is trying to see how cheap they can get you no matter where you're looking, so just ask for more.

They're not going to take your job away, so if you ask for an increase of 10 percent, they'll either just say no or maybe they'll say, "Okay how about five percent?" There's a way to make your request where you're simultaneously communicating the message that you're willing to advocate for yourself and that you'll use those skills to advocate for their company in your new job position. Plus, even if they only come up a thousand or two a year, if you do that every time you move jobs, that's a lot of money over time.

Good luck finding the courage to not be so timid,
Betches

4.

ANY UPDATES HERE?

I Have a Job, Now What?

Congrats, you have a job!

Also, sorry. Welcome to the stressful and unpredictable world of adulthood. For the recent college graduate, there's literally nothing worse than the transition from having one college class a day to having a legitimate full-time job that you're required to be at for eight-plus hours every single day. We've always thought that there should be some sort of formal transition year where you slowly build up to a true full-time schedule over several months, but unfortunately, the fundamental patterns of the American economy are not up to us. Weird, right? If you think about it, it's really strange how one day you're getting drunk at 2:00 p.m. on a Wednesday with your college roommates, and the next you're spending two hours a day commuting to a cubicle with extremely unflattering fluorescent lighting and coworkers who say shit like "Happy Tuesday."

One of the starkest differences you'll experience is the vast change in social dynamics between the earlier phases of your life and true, working adulthood. Sure, you may have had internships in the past, but a lot of the time these were either total bullshit jobs where you could wear your sunglasses all day, or if they actually were legit, you were still just an ~~indentured servant~~ intern and therefore standards were generally lower. It's hard for anyone to scrutinize your work ethic when you're basically just

> You know what the weirdest part about having a job is? You have to be there every day. Even on the days you don't feel like it.
>
> —Jessa, *Girls*

getting coffee for everyone at your unpaid internship. Even if you interned somewhere serious and awful like an investment bank, you still knew that the light at the end of the tunnel that was fall semester was only twelve short weeks away. Real life is different because your actions have consequences that follow you and affect your reputation in the long term, meaning that your performance is not just relevant to your current job but can potentially impact future jobs you may want to get in your industry. Also, there is no end in sight to the 6:00 a.m. wakeups, and your shitty boss isn't going anywhere until one of you gets a new job or is fired. It's not like high school or college where if you're having a bad year, at least there's a specific end date. Your classes would be over at the end of the semester and your annoying professor would finally get off your ass.

The most terrifying thing about having a real job is that unless you make some serious moves to change your life and your job, what you're doing today could be the same thing you're doing ten years from now . . . unless you plan to quit after having kids. Finally, a socially acceptable advantage over men.

THERE'S NO PLACE LIKE COLLEGE: LEARNING THE SOCIAL NORMS OF WORK LIFE

One of the first things you figure out in your first full-time job is that the workforce has its own very specific set of unwritten rules and etiquette. For example, whereas it used to be okay to send blatantly passive-aggressive emails to your entire sorority listserv without caring who you pissed off, now it's time to learn how to use reply all in a way that doesn't leave the entire office gossiping about your "psychological issues." The first thing you need to internalize is that work etiquette is not like social etiquette, and the more you mix the two, the more likely you are to come across as unprofessional and immature. We're not saying you should *be* a different person at work, we're just saying that if your personality sucks or you're really immature, it might be necessary to fake it till you make it.

While there's definitely a spectrum of different office cultures and degrees of seriousness (read: how much you have to act like a robotic bore), the main thread across any and all professional contexts is that you will probably have to curb your negative impulses in some way, no matter where you work. There's a saying that you never truly know someone until you live with them or work with them, which speaks to how difficult it can be to interact professionally in many circumstances. After graduating college and finishing a summer of doing nothing but fucking around with your friends, it's never going to be harder to just switch off your fun, blackout-every-Thursday summer self and switch on your fake pantsuit persona.

The biggest distinction between social norms and work norms is the extent to which you want to attract attention. Within your friend group, obviously you want to find yourself at the center of as much excitement as possible, be that brunch plans or a bachelorette party. At work, etiquette can basically be boiled down to one major rule when it comes to complying with norms, and it's the polar opposite of your social life: Never be the narrative.

We know that sometimes the narrative can be a really good thing in the context of like, actual achievements. What we mean by being the narrative here is that you don't want to be the *problem*. Having an achievement means you have moments. Moments are good because you get a flash of positivity, success, and a reputation boost. This is very different from being the narrative, which means being the central thread of drama.

Ever notice how the woman who wins *The Bachelor* never carries the drama throughout multiple episodes? (Yes, Courtney Robertson is an exception; we are *Bachelor* scholars.) Sure, the winner has cute dates and you know she's a front-runner the whole time, but the winner is never that intriguing or interesting, and she usually isn't part of the central conflict. If you're trying to figure out how to navigate the new world of how to act at work, you are aiming to give yourself the edit that *Bachelor* producers give the inevitable winner. Don't try to be the popular girl at the office. Get noticed for your achievements, not for your drunk stories from the weekend. Be the Becca K., not the Krystal.

How? Basically, try to lay low and put your best efforts forward while looking like you're working hard, at least until you've figured out the dynamic of your new office. Take note of what other seemingly well-respected people are doing, and don't cross any lines that you aren't 100 percent sure they would cross. Try to get a sense of the hierarchy, and don't fuck with anybody or talk shit about them until you know you would be safe in doing so.

It all sounds very *Game of Thrones*, but it's important to

consider all things, like alliances and power dynamics. Save your dramatic tendencies for roasting people in your friend group chat on your lunch break.

OFFICE POLITICS AND WORK DYNAMICS: HOW TO DEAL

Something that often gets lost in all the motivational quotes, inspirational career advice, and bullshit lunch-and-learns about how to "set goals for success" is that many of our experiences at work are not necessarily in our control. Scary, we know. Often, so much of what women deal with throughout our careers is really about the people we encounter and how we relate to them, for better or worse. Most of the time, we hear about how other people can impact our career in the context of mentorship or networking, but the less commonly held conversation is about the importance of your coworkers. That's right, the people you deal with every day, who you have literally no choice but to suck it up and interact with, no matter how you feel about them.

Me to my best friends: Ugh I seriously hate people so much.

Me applying for jobs: I love working with people and I'm very sociable.

Your coworker situation can make or break a job experience. Even a really lame job that pays nothing can be made tolerable by having cool people around. The opposite is also true though, and if you hate everyone you work with or have no connection to anyone, a job that's good on paper can become really miz in reality.

THE FIVE PEOPLE YOU MEET ~~IN HELL~~ AT WORK AND HOW TO DEAL WITH THEM

You're going to come across lots of different people throughout your career, but there are definitely a few distinct personality types you'll encounter no matter where you go or what industry you're in. Figuring out which type you're working with and how to deal with them can be just as critical to your success as learning how to properly word a passive-aggressive refrigerator note.

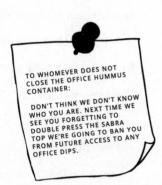

TO WHOMEVER DOES NOT CLOSE THE OFFICE HUMMUS CONTAINER:

DON'T THINK WE DON'T KNOW WHO YOU ARE. NEXT TIME WE SEE YOU FORGETTING TO DOUBLE PRESS THE SABRA TOP WE'RE GOING TO BAN YOU FROM FUTURE ACCESS TO ANY OFFICE DIPS.

The Try Hard

Think Tracy Flick, Hermione Granger in the early books, Warner Huntington III's new fiancée. We all know her. She practically enters your boss's asshole as her shipping address when she shops online. Both a social climber and an overachiever, she's the worst combination possible. She's the one organizing her desk drawer by paper clip size and correcting your grammar in a casual work email. There's nothing more to really say about her because we're all on the same page and we're all already picturing someone we know.

HOW TO DEAL: Stay far away when you don't need her for anything; be nice to her when you do. There's no need to be too close to someone who bothers you unless you absolutely have to be, and if you need her help with something, she'll probably do a really good job. But other than that, you should stay away because she's likely a competitive little bitch and you definitely don't need that stress in your life.

Keeping that in mind, always be nice and neutral toward this person because chances are high that she has a good relationship with higher management (remember, the bosses don't call her a Try Hard, they call her Employee of the Month), and you don't want her undermining you because of a random personal vendetta about the time she was in the bathroom stall next to you when you were talking shit about her to your work bestie.

The Hot Mess

Think Meredith Palmer, Carrie Mathison, Lindsay Lohan on the set of any movie. Pretty much the opposite of the Try Hard, the Hot Mess is probably the most fun person at the office. She always goes the hardest at happy hour, always seems to be in a slight daze of hangover and Vyvanse, and always has entertaining stories about how she ended up hooking up with a *Bachelorette* contestant at 4:00 a.m. the night before. On a work night! At the same time, she tends to be likable and basically competent enough to avoid getting fired. She's probably hooked up with multiple coworkers and dedicates most of her time to cultivating an encyclopedic knowledge of office gossip.

HOW TO DEAL: This person is perfect to have fun and get drunk with at happy hour, but never get too close to her or tell her anything too personal, especially not about anything that you wouldn't want everyone else at work knowing. We also wouldn't rely on her too much when it comes to actual work tasks, because she might not do the most amazing job, and you def don't need to be blamed for that.

The Outsider

Think Creed from The Office, *Gilfoyle from* Silicon Valley, *the Asian girl in* Pitch Perfect. No one really knows what's up with this person. She doesn't really speak to many people or share her personal life. Your feelings toward her are likely neutral with a slight bend toward thinking she's sort of weird.

She keeps to herself, does her job, and that's that . . . who does that? It's almost like she has a concept of professional boundaries or something. She might be socially awkward, she might just be shy; either way, it's not your problem.

HOW TO DEAL: This is actually one of the better characters at work because he or she doesn't really affect you. Having one less person to potentially annoy you is always a plus. Work with them when you have to, shoot them a fake smile when you don't.

The Regular Person You Are Just Chill With

Think Pam Beasley, Marnie Michaels. They're at work, you're at work. That's pretty much where the commonalities end, but you can tell she's a chill, normal person, so you just have a friendly but distant relationship. Maybe he or she is in a different office clique, and your feelings toward them are mostly neutral trending positive.

HOW TO DEAL: You don't really need to deal with her unless you have to do some actual work with her, and so you can just talk about work and pretend to care where she's going for Christmas vacation for two seconds before you dive into those TPS reports.

Your Work Wife

Think Meredith and Cristina, Ross Geller and his monkey. Your work wife is the person who makes it worth staying at your job. You're actually friends outside of work, you side text during all conference calls, and she basically gets you through those brutal 9:00-to-4:55 days.

HOW TO DEAL: With your work wife, it's probably best if your actual jobs are as nonintertwined as possible, while still giving you opportunities to work together occasionally. You definitely want to avoid conflict with your work wife, since you would be bored and miserable without her. Plus, everyone already knows you're friends and will definitely notice the tension, and then you have to explain that you drunkenly hooked up with her brother at a bar this past weekend and now she's kind of pissed about it. Try to get staffed together on projects, but only once in a while.

FIGURING OUT YOUR OFFICE CULTURE AND HOW TO ACT IN IT

This is one of the hardest topics for us to give specific advice on because every industry has different standards of what they consider okay. What totally flies in some office cultures might be literal career suicide in another. So observe your surroundings while remembering to never become the narrative. The way you figure out what you can get away with is pretty much completely dependent on what everyone else is doing. Figure out what the norms are and then navigate them so that you are never the fuckup. For example, if dancing on top of a bar makes you the narrative in one job but is totally okay, or even encouraged, in another, then go ahead and sing "Baby Back Ribs" at the top of your lungs all you want at the office holiday party. Just hope nobody puts it on their Instagram story.

Happy Hours, Retreats, and Work Events: How Drunk Should I Get?

Simple: Always be slightly less drunk than everyone around you and sober enough to ensure that you won't find yourself vomiting, revealing secrets (personal or work-related) to anyone around you, bitching out your boss or coworkers, or publicly hooking up with the IT guy in the middle of the bar. Even if you're off-hours on a work trip or retreat, and even if your office is not a regular office—it's a cool office—that only flies up to a certain point. And that certain point is whatever point HR has to get involved.

As anyone who follows the Betches office on Instagram stories knows, we don't exactly have the most rigid atmosphere when it comes to partying. At the same time, we know there's a line, and if you can't handle drinking without acting like a high school freshman taking her first shot of Malibu, you need to get your shit together. Here are some things we would consider okay and not okay in the context of partying at work events.

It's okay to . . .	It's not okay to . . .
Take shots with your boss.	Take shots at your boss.
Ignore your work emails for the night.	Write your boss a typo-filled email telling them to shove their feedback up their ass.
Start pregaming happy hour at 4:30.	Start pregaming happy hour at 1:30.
Do karaoke.	Do your married coworker in the bathroom.
Buy a shot for your coworkers on your company credit card.	Buy shots for the entire bar on your company credit card.
Throw up when you get home.	Throw up in public.
Show up a little later than usual the next day.	Show up later than your first meeting.

See, there's a line. Don't cross it.

Cautionary Betchy Tale:
The Thinx Sexual Harassment Lawsuit

Miki Agrawal was the founder and CEO of Thinx, a company that makes "period underwear" and is known for their scandalous NYC subway ads. Miki had a desire to make her company ultrafeminist and create an extremely open, liberal environment, which is amazing, and we're all for that. However, an ex-employee alleged that Miki was doing some batshit-crazy things for the sake of trying to keep things loose. Chelsea Leibow, Miki's former head of publicity, accused her of touching employees' breasts, changing clothes in front of them, shaming women for asking for raises, expressing sexual interest in her employees, and introducing "culture queens" instead of HR.

While we can't comment on the validity of these claims, the Thinx lawsuit is a cautionary reminder that no matter what kind of progressive, fun office you may work for, it's absolutely essential that you remain professional at work.

You may think your coworkers are your friends, but in an office environment, certain kinds of fucking around may be misconstrued, make people uncomfortable, and may even be illegal. Like if you think you're on a close enough level with your work BFF that you could call her a "ho" in a reply all to an email chain and it would be hysterical, you are definitely wrong. If you're not sure if something is appropriate, err on the side of caution. The last thing you need is for something you meant as a joke to be used against you and hinder your growth and success. Remember that what you grew up assuming was appropriate to say may not be the case for other people and may actually be highly offensive to them. Think Karen Smith asking Cady why she's white. Work can be fun (sort of), but above all, it should create an environment where people feel comfortable enough to say if they feel like something is inappropriate or if someone's behavior is getting in the way of productivity.

Office Dress Codes: Dress to Impress, Not for Your Ex

When it comes to work clothes, every situation is different. It varies from office to office depending on the culture, who works there, the industry you're in, even what city you work in. While it used to be that women had to wear skirt suits, hose, and high heels to work every day, we're now living in a whole different world. The wardrobe of a CEO can consist of hoodies and socks with sandals (giving Russian bots all our data is clearly not Mark Zuckerberg's only crime against humanity). Lucky for us, we get to take a cue from that and no longer have to spend an additional $5,000 a year on fugly biz-casual wear from Loft that has literally no use outside the office. But that doesn't mean that standards are totally gone, they're just a little less clearly defined. So how do you know what to wear?

Just "dress to impress," by which we mean in a professional way, not to show off how hot you can potentially look. Save that lewk for the weekend and your vacation instas. Even if everyone agrees that you're like, really pretty and you want to emphasize that, there's a way to go about it without putting your appearance front and center. This is work, not a beauty pageant or your fashion blog (unless your work is a beauty pageant or a fashion blog, in which case skip this section).

Figuring out the right way to dress for your job is pretty much a combination of taking cues from your coworkers and common sense. If you want to avoid any potential mistakes, dress on a similar level of formality to how everyone else is dressed so you don't stand out. You should always lean toward conservative and aim for people to ignore your looks as much as possible. (We know, societal standards for when women are not allowed to look hot versus when we are required to look hot are like, so fickle.) By no means are we suggesting that you shouldn't try to look pretty, or your best, or hide your entire body in a tentlike outfit. But don't lead with your appearance. Unlike what we believed in college, it's actually possible to look really great even while not revealing everything.

As women we deal with enough criticism for stupid shit, like overusing the word *like* and being considered entitled because we want equal wages, so the last thing you need is to create another problem for yourself in the form of your boss thinking you're trying to get ahead using your sexuality. It's more than okay to express yourself, but the reality is that there are boundaries to what appropriate expression is at work.

The truth is that avoiding getting labeled inappropriate is pretty simple: if you're questioning whether something you want to wear is inappropriate, just don't wear it. Save it for brunch or a date. If your slutty outfit is the only clean one you have right now, you can also text your work wife an #ootd mirror pic in the morning before you leave and ask her thoughts, but just be careful who you ask. For example, we would not recommend surveying your friend who regularly wears a bodysuit with cutouts, crop tops, or smoky eyes to work, no matter how liberal you think your office atmosphere is. Be sure to ask someone who dresses appropriately themselves and who you know won't screenshot your text and send it around to half the office with a caption: *LOLOL can you believe Amanda almost wore this!?*

If you ever have a meeting at another office or someone new is coming in for a meeting, that's the time to be extra careful. Just because your boss is chill with your work-to-gym athleisure situation doesn't mean that your potential client is. You never know who you could meet in a work context on any given day or what bad impressions you could accidentally be making with your outfit. Do you really need to deal with the extra work of undoing that impression just because you wanted to wear a slightly lower-cut shirt one day? If you said yes, you should probably reprioritize.

We're not saying this is how the rules should be, but this is how it is, and it's much better for your own long-term benefit to acknowledge it. We somehow doubt that on the day you ask for a raise you'll be regretting the fact that no one at the office got to see your new belly button ring.

One of the reasons it's a good idea to dress appropriately and lean toward the more conservative side is that if you ever find yourself in a situation where you don't feel totally comfortable or have doubts about your outfit choice, it will probably affect your confidence in that moment. Ever notice how you feel when you realize you're under- or overdressed for a situation like a date or a party? You probably fidget a lot subconsciously, play with your clothes, and generally feel distracted. You already probably have some degree of ADD, and it's even harder to stay present and be at peak performance when you're wondering if people are staring at your Power-Point slide or your bra sliding out of your shirt. Again, shit is hard enough for women at work, and the last thing you need is some pervy guy mentally estimating your cup size when he should be estimating your company's valuation.

So figure out what your office's actual dress code is. Not

the one in the handbook, but the unspoken one. How casual is Friday, really? It's hard for us to give a specific list of dos and don'ts when it comes to dressing because what might fly in one workplace could earn you the career equivalent of a *Handmaid's Tale* stoning in another. Jeans might be totally okay in one place and a cardinal sin in another. Flip-flops or anything you would wear to the beach are generally a no across the board, although nice sandals might be okay in some places. See the handy chart for some overarching dos and don'ts.

The one rule that always applies is, regardless of the specific dress code, you should always aim to look like the most-put-together version of what's allowed. Let's say you're working at one of those super-casual offices where hoodies are normal. That is not a cue to dress like a slob. Your hoodie should be clean and free of the remains of yesterday's happy hour guac on the sleeve. Same goes for super-dressy offices like law firms, where a lot of people wear skirts, dresses, and heels. Make sure your heels are clean and don't have bar-floor remnants from this past weekend on them. When it comes to makeup, there's a reason why there are day looks and night looks. If you want to wear a bold matte lip, go light on the eyes, and vice versa. It's also less to worry about in terms of constantly wondering if your eyeliner is smudged or your bronzer is all over your white top.

what to wear
OFFICE EDITION

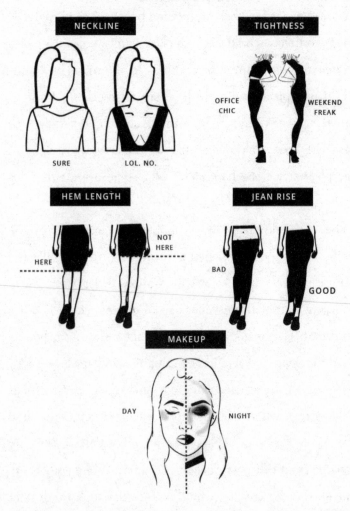

Last, allow yourself to be comfortable. While you'll never achieve Sunday-on-the-couch-level comfort, don't wear things that you'll have to be fixing all day, like shirts that won't stay tucked in or skirts that ride up. Make sure your clothes fit and your button-down shirt isn't busting open every time you make a hand gesture.

If any of this is unclear, we've designed an easy guide for those of you who are more visual and need examples (see opposite). And if you've already been doing it wrong, don't worry, you don't need to go find a new job where they've never seen your fishnet stockings before. You're allowed to make mistakes and you're allowed to get better. You're just not allowed to wear a vest, because that vest was disgusting.

How to Speak Like a Mature Adult and Not Sound Like You're at a Sorority Chapter

Bad news: people you encounter in work environments are not always going to assume the best about you. Specifically, one of the biggest things people—especially older people—judge at work is the way you speak, so you should probably get comfortable using legal jargon in everyday life, or whatever.

Since it's one of very few aspects of yourself that's completely within your control, you definitely don't want the way you speak to put you at a disadvantage. As a woman, in many situations your superiors are probably already automatically judging everything you say. We seriously wish we were kidding. The last things you need when trying to establish yourself in the workplace are blank stares and secret convos about your verbal tics.

Good news: though you may sound like a sorority girl on a cocaine binge when you're feeling enthusiastic, there are ways to make yourself sound more like a normal person, or at least what old people would consider normal. Just the facts.

Here are some verbal habits that you should train yourself to avoid.

Using the word *like*: We know, eliminating *like* means knocking out like, half the total words you say, period. Same here. But if you—like us—cringe every time you hear yourself on a recording, you'll probably notice that saying *like* more often than you say literally any other word makes you sound like Cher Horowitz in debate class. Sure, she got her C+ all the way to an A solely based on her powers of persuasion, but *Clueless* is a movie, she was in high school, and your boss is not going to be manipulated into giving you a raise because you set him up on a date with Susan in accounting.

Vocal fry: One of those terms used most frequently by people who write articles about how millennials have killed the napkin industry, *vocal fry* basically just means making your voice sound very low-pitched and making a sort of creaking, dragging sound in some of your words. Think of how you speak when you're slumped over on your couch scrolling through Instagram and your boyfriend asks you what you want for dinner and you're like, *"Iiiiii dunnoooo what dyouuuu wantttt???"* Even to our still-youthful ears, it's incredibly annoying and unprofessional, so please try to stop doing this. Practically speaking, we know it's really hard to fix because no one sounds the same to themselves as they do to everyone else. The best way to go about this would probably be to record yourself speaking on a phone call for about twenty minutes (or long enough to forget that you're being recorded so it actually sounds like your usual self), then force yourself to listen to it after so you can hear the types of words and sentences you use it in, and then try to concentrate on not doing it next time you're bored in a conversation; it'll give you something more interesting to focus on while speaking to someone you're not in the mood to talk to. Think of it as an accent-change exercise. But don't make it worse: cough, Dorit Kemsley, cough.

Upspeak: This just means making your voice go up at the end of sentences, effectively making all your statements sound like questions and making you sound like you're unsure of everything you say. Nothing undermines you more than turning all your statements into questions, so it sounds like you're always asking permission or apologizing for what you think. Even if you're not 100 percent sure of yourself or what you're saying (which is okay because if you're always 100 percent sure, everyone else probably thinks you're a know-it-all beyotch), it's a good idea to act like you're fairly sure of yourself (without sounding overconfident; naturally, as a woman you must always walk that fine line between being too much and not enough for people. Rant over). Be sure of yourself and try to make your sentences sound like they have a period at the end of them. Like we recommended for getting rid of vocal fry, it helps to listen to yourself speaking

> Speak in statements instead of apologetic questions.
>
> —Tina Fey, *Bossypants*

to hear what you're doing wrong and then designate times to focus on speaking without those annoying tics. The key is to do it frequently for short spurts of time, as opposed to one day of paying attention to it and then forgetting about it. Nothing changes overnight, especially not something as ingrained as your own vocal patterns.

Speaking before you know what you want to say: Unless your boss is literally staring you in the face asking you for an answer to a specific question, you never need to feel rushed to speak. You're not Oprah (unless you are Oprah—hi, thanks for reading), and in most situations, no one is just dying to hear what you have to say next. And if you're the kind of person who regularly says something dumb or unclear before you really think it through, people are going to draw the conclusion that you don't know what you're talking about and will be more likely to discount what you have to say in the future. If you don't know something and don't want to sound like an idiot, you can say, "Let me think about it and get back to you," which will make people think you are thoughtful and measured. It's a great quality for people to think you have. No one has to know how stupid or unprepared you are until you open your mouth and tell them yourself.* So just keep your mouth shut and let them assume you're a genius.

Speaking too quickly: This goes especially for when you're excited about something, because then you end up looking like the Charlie from *It's Always Sunny* conspiracy theory meme. You know the one. It's really good to be passionate about what you're doing, but it's probably best to demonstrate that through hard work, going above and beyond your responsibilities, and

---

* The exception to this is if you're in a managerial or director position and rarely say anything at all, in which case your bosses will start to wonder why they hired you in the first place. If you want to say less, that's fine, but make sure that when they hear you speak you're discussing some plan that's productive and relevant to a work project instead of your personal life or the recent plot of *The Real Housewives of New Jersey.*

always doing a thorough job, rather than having what appears to be a manic episode during a meeting. The best way to stop doing this is to try to notice when you're getting excited (increasing heart rate, feeling your face turning red), and make it a habit to take a full deep breath every time before you start speaking and in between long sentences. If breathing is hard for you, we recommend meditating for five to ten minutes a day (like, actually meditating and not just zoning out thinking about a guy and then bragging to everyone about how Zen you are). You should notice an improvement in a few weeks, and if you actually commit to doing it, it will help you learn how to breathe properly and also help you generally calm the fuck down.

Going around in circles: This goes along with speaking before you know what you're saying. A lot of bad salespeople do this, where they choose two to three buzzwords and use them to speak out of their asses. Even worse, sometimes that speech goes on for five whole minutes, so much so that at the end of it, everyone on the conference call feels like they need a vacation. Being a bullshitter requires actual bullshitting skills. Make a point to end your sentence. Even if your point isn't based on anything, as long as everyone else thinks it is, you're in the clear. During a conversation, it's very transparent when someone doesn't know what their point is and is constantly running around a hamster wheel trying to find it.

So how do you actually implement these changes? It's not easy, but trying to be self-aware and to notice when you're doing these things will help, at least to start. Then when you try to pay attention and practice not doing them, they should start to diminish and hopefully eventually disappear. Think of it as working out, but for your voice.

A NOTE ON CRYING AT WORK

What kind of monsters would we be if we didn't address the ultimate taboo topic: crying at work.

Crying gets a reputation as a signifier of weakness, lack of control over emotions, incompetence, and dare we say it . . . femininity. That's where phrases such as "boys don't cry" and "cry like a girl" come from, fucking duh. Crying at work is associated with not being boss-like, not owning your position, not being able to suck it up, and other vaguely masculine-coded behaviors. So while we don't encourage crying as your sole approach to handling stress, we also realize that the vilification of crying is one of those subtle biases against women at work. And for that reason, we have to defend your right to cry . . . in private, when no one is looking, outside of work hours.

Personally, we recommend waiting until you get home to cry for the sake of saving yourself potential embarrassment and having to deal with your mascara running. Also, the bathroom line is getting long and everyone knows it's you in there. Still, don't let people tell you you're weak because you cry. As much as people hate on crying, crying is shadily amazing. It's a very healthy way of releasing emotions, as opposed to, let's say, bingeing on food, alcohol, or shopping. Everyone feels better after crying, and it's a naturally human way to cope with stress and process feelings.

Like we said, while it's better to cry when you get home, the truth is that everyone cries at work from time to time. If you've never cried at your actual office, maybe you've gone home and cried about something that happened that day (the preferred timing). Either way, crying about your job means you care about it, and that is always preferable to doing a job you DGAF about. Think about it, people cry when they have personal/family/ friend situations that are stressful, and that's because those things and/or people are important to them. If you want success, that means your career is important to you, and stress is inevitable, unless it's just that your boss is a total bitch. Having something to cry about means having something to care about, and that's definitely a place you want to be at in your career.

NETWORKING: IT'S LIKE DATING FOR PROFESSIONAL GAIN

Ugh, networking. No one wants to do it, everyone has to. TBH, though, the few times we've legitimately put forth effort into networking, good things have always come out of it. Everyone knows it's uncomfortable, and once you've accepted that, you can finally figure out how to do it well.

Depending on what your particular job is, sometimes networking is not really necessary unless you want to find a new job, which we addressed earlier. But now we're going to talk about how to network for your current job. Sometimes networking is pretty much a requirement to gain new clients or spread the word on whatever it is your company is doing. And if you're thinking that this doesn't apply to you, guess what, internal networking is also a thing that can help you improve your overall job situation and standing at the company you're in (especially if it's a large corporation where you don't regularly work closely with everyone already). There's a clear goal you should be going for in all of your networking interactions, no matter if they're internal or external to your workplace. It's better to be known and liked than known and not liked; if you're not going to be liked, better to not be known.

This seems obvious in theory (duh, who doesn't want to either be loved or go into hiding?), but in action it takes some real self-awareness. If you know you're bad at small talk, which is pretty much the cornerstone of networking, then just get fucking better at it, or figure out how to fake it. It's really not that hard. Most people who say they're bad at small talk (a.k.a. all three of us) are really saying that they don't give a shit about people who they don't already care about, usually for some relatively selfish reason. Do you just have soooo much trouble remembering people's names? Yeah, that's because you don't give a shit about that person. Think about it: Have you ever forgotten Beyoncé's name? No! That's because when you care about someone, you don't forget their name.

So while we agree it's annoying as fuck to actually be present and engaged IRL conversations with randos when you could be stalking different randos on Instagram, if you want to be more successful at your career, it's going to involve doing a lot of things that you don't really "feel like" doing, and this is one of them. So act like you care what Karen from HR might be talking about, and maybe even actually care a little bit, and the next time you're up for a promotion, somehow mysteriously HR is on board.

The keys to networking are basically (1) being present in conversations, (2) remembering people's names, and (3) appearing useful. We once read a tip in *Forbes* or somewhere that if you repeat people's names back to them, it not only makes them like you more but it generally makes you more likely to remember their name. And you know how much you love to talk about yourself? Well guess what, so does everyone else, so give them the opportunity to do so. Ask the other person open-ended questions about themselves that give them a chance to talk about themselves and keep the conversation going, giving you more commentary you can work with to ask more questions about. This not only saves you from having to expend energy on forming coherent answers to *their* questions, but it makes them remember the conversation more positively because they got to talk about their favorite topic: themselves. Try to remember how much bullshit you pretended to care about during sorority rush and channel that energy. If you have something in common, capitalize on that by saying something like, "OMG same! I loved Iceland! Weren't the waterfalls just like, sooooo pretty?" And no, it doesn't matter that you literally hated Iceland because the sandwiches were $40 each, you posted really pretty pictures, so that's barely even lying.

On the flip side, being a bad networker is pretty easy, too. I mean, all you have to do is lean into your more narcissistic tendencies and chances are you'll fuck something up. Dominating the conversation, interrupting, taking out your phone, not showing interest in what the other person has to say, and being argumentative or combative about controversial topics with someone you just met all fall into the category of things you should try to avoid. When in doubt, just shut up and excuse yourself to get another drink or go to the bathroom if you think the conversation is going south. Then hope that they weren't paying attention when you said your name. I mean, if they're anything like you, the chances are pretty high.

Now that we've talked about how to suck up to people for the sake of expanding your network, it's time to use those tactics to manage the most important person to suck up to: your boss.

DEALING WITH YOUR BOSS: TYPES OF MANAGERS AND HOW TO MANAGE *THEM*

Bitching about your boss is a sacred right. When it comes to anything that happens between nine and five on a weekday, your boss can be the one to blame. Procrastinated too much on a project and now you have to stay late to finish it? No problem, it's your boss's fault for not assigning it soon enough. Filter on the water cooler broken? Boss (well, technically, office manager, but your boss made a bad hire). It's raining outside, and you still have to go to work? Boss. Boyfriend isn't proposing? B-O-S-S. A boss is kind of like your mom that way, except instead of threatening that she won't take you on the family vacation this year, your boss can actually make a big difference in your life and fire you.

The truth is that it's human nature to hate the boss. People have been hating their bosses ever since the Garden of Eden employee handbook was written and the only policy was that they weren't allowed to eat their boss's food, which was clearly labeled in the office fridge. People still hate their bosses just as much as Adam and Eve did then, simply because they are the easiest people to blame for any misery in your life. Even though you could technically choose to stop working and slip into poverty or debt instead, most people would rather maintain the privilege of complaining about their boss.

Every job has a boss, which means that the trick is to figure out how to deal with yours. But remember: your boss is just a regular fucked-up human like everybody else, and they aren't making your life miz on purpose. Who we are at work is not some random new persona that only exists in the office. Aren't you the same person throughout your life, with some minor tweaks and maybe slightly more self-control in professional settings? The same goes for your boss. So a psycho bitch in real life will be a psycho bitch when they're your boss, and the best you can hope for is that your boss's parents didn't fuck them up too badly.

Obviously, every boss in your career is going to be different. Some people have amazing relationships with their managers, some of whom even become mentors or friends. On the other hand, some bosses are irrelevant and have little impact on your life overall. We can't possibly address every managerial relationship out there, but we can definitely narrow it down to a few stereotypes. So, what are some of the common boss personalities and how do you navigate them?

The Psycho

This is the worst boss to have, hence the term *psycho*. You've all heard the horror stories. Psychosis can reveal itself in many different ways, but generally signs of erratic behavior or moods—emotional outbursts, manic emailing, crazy spending, talking excessive shit about coworkers to you— might be signs that your boss is a psycho. This person might come off as super nice upon interviewing or when you first start the job, but then you'll start noticing a slow burn of behavior that reminds you of your Vicodin-addicted college ex. The thing to remember about the psycho boss is that they are a regular psycho in real life, they just happen to also be your boss. You're not going to change them, you just have to deal.

> **Miranda Priestly:** *You have no style or sense of fashion.*
>
> **Andy Sachs:** *I think that depends on what you're—*
>
> **Miranda Priestly:** *No, no, that wasn't a question.*
>
> —The Devil Wears Prada

HOW TO DEAL: If possible, try to look out for signs that your future boss might be a psycho before you even accept a job offer. Try to observe the way their underlings act around them when you go in for your interviews. Does everyone look like they're freaking the fuck out? Then, yeah, this person might be a horror film embodied. Maybe don't take that job, or if you can, reach out to people at the company and ask how they feel about working there. If they blink twice, run.

Let's say you don't really have the option of being choosy with your job, or you know that a particular position will be beneficial to your overall career advancement and specific aspirations. So you go work for this person even though you suspect a psycho. The first step is acceptance that the person you're working for is who they are and that you can't really do much to change them, outside of secretly slipping a therapist's business card into their desk. *OMG, no, Joan, I have no idea who put that there!* Seriously, though, dealing with this type of person every day can take a real toll on your mental health if it's bad enough, so we recommend trying to get away from such a person as soon as possible. Whether this means getting reassigned within the company or finding a new job altogether, this should probably be your goal.

In the meantime, figure out what sets them off and do not do those things. Observe how other people fuck up and then do the exact opposite of that. Keep your head down, do your job well, and try not to give them things to come after you for. We understand that you're dealing with an unstable person, so this is probably much easier said than done, but most of what you're doing will probably involve managing your relationship with this person. The key is to figure out what sets them off (probably everything, but focus on the main things) and avoid doing those things like you would a bro with syphilis. At the same time, psychos are capable of being happy or pleased with things, so figuring out what those things are would probably be a good idea. From there it's a simple equation: Do more of the things they like, do less of the things they don't. This is the only way to potentially make your situation more bearable while you work on permanently getting away from them.

The Micromanager

The micromanager is one of the most annoying bosses to come by and one of the most common . . . but not the worst. The micromanager is probably just an anxious control freak in their personal life and can't help but let it bleed into their management style. They'll sit on top of everything you do, nitpick emails you send that they're cc'ed on even though the task is already completed, make you do a thousand drafts of the same thing with very slight changes, and just generally won't trust you to do any motherfucking thing without their express approval.

HOW TO DEAL: Just deal until you can get promoted or find a new job, or some other way out of having them be your immediate supervisor. Or maybe do a specific project with a very faraway deadline to completion and surprise them by proving that you can actually do something with very little feedback. If that doesn't change anything, the one thing to remember is that their micromanagement is not necessarily about your incompetence (although it can be, and it's totally up to you to figure out how to be a better employee, which we'll get to later), it's about their own shit and their inability to relinquish control. If you absolutely can't get away from this person or avoid them, do everything in your power to make sure you're following your boss's specific instructions and even go a step further by asking yourself, "What is the next thing he or she

> *Stan, Chotchkie's manager: We need to talk about your flair.*
>
> *Joanna: Really? I . . . I have fifteen pieces on. I, also—*
>
> *Stan: Well, okay. Fifteen is the minimum, okay?*
>
> *Joanna: Okay.*
>
> *Stan: Now, you know it's up to you whether or not you want to just do the bare minimum. Or, uh . . . well, like Brian, for example, has thirty-seven pieces of flair on today, okay. And a terrific smile.*
>
> —Office Space

is going to ask me to do after I show them this?" If you just *know* there's going to be another round of corrections or a next step, maybe do that in advance, or craft two versions of something so that you can show them options. Micromanagers ultimately just want to feel like they're in control and that people are pleasing them, so the more thorough you are, the less they will be able to micromanage.

The Incompetent

How this person even became a manager is extremely unclear. Did they sleep with someone? Was it a timing thing? Blackmail? Regardless, somehow this person is now above you in the hierarchy, and you're going to have to figure out how to deal with it. One of the biggest problems with having a direct manager who is incompetent is that at some point or another, you're probably going to get blamed for their mistakes or bad communication, and it might be difficult to pin it back on them.

HOW TO DEAL: Take one for the team and correct their shit, but don't make too big of a scene about doing so. Who knows, maybe you can get promoted above them. Chances are that if they're *that* incompetent, other people are aware of it and feel bad for you. Use this to your advantage to show everyone how amazing you are at coming through in bad circumstances and do everything you can to turn this into a chance to get ahead.

The Sexual Assailant

Hopefully there are going to be fewer of these in the future, but for now, let's talk about it. The iconic alleged sexual assailant is obviously Harvey Weinstein (we say *alleged* because our legal team made us), but he's probably the most extreme example, and lots of behaviors can fall into this category without involving literal rape or assault. (See: Miki Agrawal in the section about office culture, page 118.) This is the boss whose gaze lingers a little too long on your cleavage, touches you just a *little* too inappropriately (TBH, no boss should ever be touching you for any reason), arranges reasons for you to be alone together, makes offhand comments about your coworkers' looks or the length of your skirt or how nice your smile is. You get a bad feeling from them, and you don't need to actually be assaulted to be able to intuit that someone is

> *My Indian culture seminar was going great, until Toby decided that he was too immature to deal with culturally explicit images. It's just sex, people! Everybody does it! I'm doing it with Carol . . . probably tonight!*
>
> —Michael Scott, *The Office*

being super creepy. I mean, you've been to a frat house, and if your boss's behavior reminds you of a "CEOs and Corporate Hoes" mixer, you know you've found yourself in the office of the sexual-assailant boss.

HOW TO DEAL: Tell HR. This might not have worked as effectively without hard evidence in the past, but thanks to the #MeToo era, companies are now extremely careful about sexual harassment and don't want to go anywhere near a controversy. If you're afraid to go to HR because you're worried that your boss won't actually be fired or moved within the company and you'll be stuck with him knowing you reported him, there are actual laws against that shit. They're called retaliation laws, and you can either google them or you can pay a lawyer $800 an hour to explain them to you, but basically it means that if you report someone for sexual harassment or discrimination and then they do something to negatively impact you after the fact, like not giving you a deserved raise or even being an asshole to you (i.e., they "retaliate," get it?), the company can get in even more trouble than for the original indiscretion. The justice system, so just right now.

> *Chandler: I didn't want to be the guy who has a problem with his boss slapping his bottom.*
>
> *Monica: I gotta tell ya, I think it's okay to be that guy.*
>
> —Friends

The Lazy Boss

The lazy boss loves to delegate, but not because he or she is responsible and has an amazing understanding of how to manage an organization, it's because they just don't want to do it themselves. And who can blame them? Larry David in *Curb Your Enthusiasm* taught us that there's no greater joy than foisting something onto other people, and it makes total sense that there are a lot of people in management who want to take advantage of this situation. You know you have the lazy boss when you commonly observe them asking you or others to do extremely simple tasks, not really paying attention in meetings or remembering what happened in previous meetings, or asking you questions that they could easily google or search for in their inbox. They also tend to have a lot of "weddings" to go to that they have to leave on Thursday nights for, or they're usually one of the last people in the office and one of the first people out. There are signs. Fucking read them.

> Every week I'm supposed to take four hours and do a quality spot-check at the paper mill. And of course the one year I blow it off, this happens.
>
> —Creed, *The Office*

HOW TO DEAL: Do what they want you to do, cover for them, and then use all that extra shit you did to make the argument that you deserve a promotion and a raise later on. This will be especially effective if your boss has a boss who you also work with and you're able to show how much slack you pick up. Trust us, their boss isn't oblivious to their laziness, you just have to exploit that dynamic by doing a good job.

The Good Boss

Once or twice in your life—but hopefully more—you might end up getting lucky and having like, a regular person as your manager. We don't really need to describe them too in depth because, just like the girl who got engaged very prematurely, when you know, you know.

HOW TO DEAL: IDK, write that you're happy you have a good boss in your gratitude journal every day? Be a good employee? You don't really have to deal with a good boss so much as capitalize on the situation by turning them into something of a mentor and doing a good job so that they will go to bat for you for promotions, raises, and future references. If you can't make the most of this unicorn situation, we can't help you and you're probably a shitty employee (see the following).

BE HONEST WITH YOURSELF:
ARE YOU A SHITTY EMPLOYEE?

If you're trying to get promoted or advance in any significant way in your career, one of the most important qualities to culti-vate is self-awareness, and the ability to self-evaluate and figure out where you need improvement. And then actually do those things, obviously. One of the hardest things in life is seeing your own flaws, but you have to see them before you can admit to them, and you have to admit to them in order to change them.

Before you reject the idea of looking at your less-than-amazing qualities, ask yourself a very important would-you-rather ques-tion: Would you rather never have to see anything that's wrong with you but never get promoted, get a raise, or advance in a job, *or* feel really awful about yourself for a little bit while you figure out what's wrong but ultimately become much more suc-cessful and make more money in the future? If you picked the first option, you should just give up on this book now. Thanks for buying; you wasted your money. But we have a feeling that most people reading this would pick the second option.

Here are some ways to go about finding your flaws and really understanding what they are.

Actually pay attention at your employee evals: If you want to know what your boss thinks of you, unshockingly, all you have to do is just pay attention at your yearly (or whatever) evaluation. Your boss is literally forced to formally rate your strengths and weaknesses on paper, so like, don't just let that be a wasted half hour. If they say you take too long to answer emails and it pisses clients off, just like . . . respond faster. Most of the time, the answers to fixing your shortcomings will be spelled out for you if you're willing to be open enough to listen to feedback and change habits.

Ask a coworker who isn't catty and whose opinion you respect for honest feedback: This is pretty hard because it requires being a bit vulnerable, and we're not saying you should definitely do this unless you're sure that the person you're asking will give worthwhile feedback. Otherwise you just put yourself out there for no gain, and we can hardly think of anything worse than that. The person you ask should be a little more experienced and higher up in the office, and they should be someone who is widely seen as hardworking and drama-avoidant. The last thing you need is someone gossiping about your vulnerable moments to the entire break room.

Ask your friends and family: As much as we want to think that we can put on a flawless act at work, that's really not possible. Like we mentioned earlier, who we are in life is who we are at work, just with a little more polish. You might be a little better at faking it with your coworkers than with your boyfriend, but the fundamental flaws themselves will probably be the same. If you really can't be organized enough to ever get to brunch on time, chances are that you're also disorganized at work and tend to be late to meetings or whatever. Take some cues from your weekend self, as explained by loved ones, and ask yourself if any of that is reflected in your job. Then work on that shit and use your personal life to practice as well. Maybe if you started getting to the restaurant in a timely fashion, you would not only piss off your friends less but also the habit will spill over into your work life and benefit you on multiple fronts.

Pay attention to what you criticize other people for: The traits we notice and critique about other people are often—surprise—actually the things we do ourselves. It's called projection, and it's really easy to detect—thanks, Freud. For example, it bothers the shit out of you how Michelle is constantly sucking up to your mutual boss and trying to undermine you and your coworkers by subtly throwing shade about everyone else. Meanwhile, you just spent a half hour plotting how you're going to make Michelle look like an idiot in the next meeting by criticizing her project and then offering to fix what she did. Sound familiar? Yeah, because you're actually doing the exact same thing that you criticize Michelle for.

Next time you hear yourself talking shit about a coworker, ask yourself if you might actually do the same thing you're calling them out for. Once you've answered yourself, you can keep bitching about them, but then change your behavior after.

We're not saying it'll be easy. Getting to know yourself and admitting your faults is honestly kind of the worst. But if you value yourself, you'll value your own self-improvement and you'll be okay with suffering a little and making changes for the sake of a better future.

HOW TO KNOW IF YOU'RE IN THE RIGHT JOB

For the purposes of this section, let's categorize job satisfaction in one of three ways: (1) get me the fuck out of here, (2) I'm down to chill here, and (3) #neverleaving. On any given day at your job, you may experience emotions from any of the categories, but whichever reminds you of your feelings toward your job on *most* days should provide some insight as to whether you're in the right place.

1. **Get me the fuck out of here:** Symptoms include waking up with zero drive or motivation to live; daydreaming about the slow, painful death of your boss and/or coworkers and/or self; feeling a sense of pointlessness or of having nothing to

look forward to ever; wishing sincerely that you could switch lives with your dog; frequently crying about/at work; having stress-induced nightmares about your job; questioning whether the job is even worth the ability to pay your rent.

2. **I'm down to chill here:** Most people fall into a situation like this. Your boss is the standard level of annoying sometimes, but your coworkers make the environment better; you want to be paid more, but overall the situation is pretty good; you're well-liked by the company without trying too hard; there are fun perks that break up the routine sometimes; you feel that you'll be promoted and given raises over time; the job looks pretty good on your résumé; the stress level is moderate but overall tolerable.

3. **#neverleaving:** A hashtag typically applied to honeymoons in the Maldives, this category means your job makes you excited when you think about it; you're doing something you always wanted to do and feel like you're good at it; you're satisfied with your compensation, your coworkers, your boss, etc.; you feel passionately about the actual duties your job entails and like you're making a difference in the results; you're growing professionally in a way that aligns with what you want for your life; your job treats you well and gives you time for your personal life.

The beauty of this category system is that each category name tells you exactly what you should do (assuming there are no barriers or other reasons not to do so). If you fall into category 1, look for a new job immediately. If category 2, then stick with it until the situation either starts to become a category 1 or 3, or until you decide you want a new opportunity (or a recruiter emails with a better situation). If you fall into category 3, consider yourself very #blessed. Stick with what you're doing and seriously invest in your success there.

NOW THAT YOU KNOW IF YOU WANT TO STAY AT YOUR JOB: INVESTING IN YOURSELF

No matter how long you plan to stay at a job, the most important thing to focus on is how to invest in that experience so that it's worth your time. Sounds like a lot of work and effort, we know. But, again, if you value yourself, you automatically care a lot about how you spend your time. And if you *have* to be at work every day, and you're getting paid to be there, there's literally no reason why you should not put in the effort to do a good job, and then get paid more to be there. Okay, so maybe you hate your boss or the company and want to conduct a personal vendetta against them by making them look bad. Sure, you do you. But in the end, you're really only hurting yourself by not trying at your job because you're wasting your time and becoming a shittier, lazier person in the process.

On the other hand, even if you feel kind of meh about what you're doing and you dislike your boss or whatever, excelling at your job is the best way to ensure that you get out of there ASAP. Take classes on the company dime so you can add a cute little Adobe Illustrator bullet point to the skills section of your résumé. Spend your lunchtime with your sad desk salad (seriously, why doesn't anyone go out to lunch here?) researching other companies or jobs you might be suited for and enjoy more. Get really good results on some lame-ass project so you can finally have a real answer to the interview question about the "one time you were challenged and persevered." That way, when you apply for a new job, at least you have something real to brag about to your potential new employer. There's no such thing as a pity hire (okay, fine, maybe for your angel investor's second cousin once removed), and no one is going to hire you just to save you from the fact that you hate your job. If you hate your job, invest in yourself in order to make yourself hirable elsewhere.

If you like your job, it's a whole different story. If you currently lucked into a work situation in which every day doesn't feel like a slow march toward death, know that this is pretty rare and you should be giving yourself three fire emojis for your amazingness at life. Now that you've decided to continue gracing your office with one full third of your time on earth (at least for that year, a.k.a. the minimum amount of time it takes for a job to ripen on a résumé), it's time to figure out how to make your already solid situation even better.

Next, try to focus on two things: (1) where you fit in professionally and how you can grow at your current job, and (2) where you ultimately want to be in a larger career sense within five years. It's important to think about what's going to happen at your next performance review, but even more important to always have the bigger picture of what you ultimately want running in the background of your mind.

The key to figuring out a path to invest in is paying attention to the needs of your job, your company, and the industry you're in. Try to look for what's missing in whatever situation you find yourself. For example, if your company has a lean staff and they are always low on avocados, and you know that you have an unrivaled knack for perfect avocado timing, you should just personally appoint yourself the avocado-getter and get the fucking avocados. Now just pretend that avocados are new age injectable fillers and you are the new age injectable filler surgeon, or whatever path you're pursuing. Find a niche you're good at, and exploit the fuck out of it.

TL;DR

Simple advice, yes, but in reality capitalizing on a skill set and an industry requires a lot of thought, effort, and commitment on your part. But if you put in the work, you can truly grow at your job and become better at it. It takes time, but you've got like, your whole life.

Dear Betches,

This question pertains more to my boyfriend, but I thought his situation could apply to other people. So here goes. . . .

My boyfriend is in his mid-twenties; let's call him Ted. He is a super-hard worker and within six months has already made major contributions to his company. For example, he's led projects to improve the AI of his company's computer programming tool and was trusted to give weekly presentations to company visitors and executives, mentor new hires, *and* train a new team lead . . . which brings me to my next point.

Ted's original team lead—we'll call him Mike—left his team a few months ago and was replaced with a new lead; we'll call him Justin. Justin is a nice guy, but Ted routinely tells me how Justin always slacks off, is constantly gaming at work, and overall just lacks leadership skills. Other teams and employees are constantly coming to Ted to ask questions over Justin, because Justin simply is not as informed.

I *do* think Ted is vastly undercompensated for his achievements. He is getting ready to ask for a well-deserved raise. But my question is this—*when Ted goes to ask for a raise, to what extent should he talk about Justin's lack of leadership, productivity, and involvement with the team?* I told Ted he should focus on his personal achievements at the company, instead of throwing Justin under the bus. I think if HR asks Ted about Justin, he can be honest, but as Ted puts it, he is "tired of doing someone's job for them [especially his boss's], while they slack off and still get the credit."

Thanks so much!

Sincerely,
Betch Better Have My (Boyfriend's) Money

Dear Boyfriend's Money,

Ted is in a super-frustrating situation. It's always annoying to be doing the bulk of the work while someone else takes credit for it. It's kind of like when your friend makes someone the maid of honor at her wedding but then you wind up having to plan the entire bachelorette party because they're ignoring all the group emails. Very unfair.

That being said, this is work, not your personal life. You can't just go off sending side texts to your boss talking shit about the MOH not pulling her weight and insisting that she should've given you the honor instead. The way your boyfriend's tact and professionalism is perceived by

his boss will go a lot further than his hard work on a few recent tasks.

When your boyfriend goes in for a raise, he should stress all the hard work he's been doing and focus on pointing out his specific actions that contributed to success on projects. By complaining about Justin, he'll just seem petty and like he's creating a diversion to lay any company setbacks on someone else. Think about how some girls on *The Bachelor* waste their time complaining about how other girls aren't there for the right reasons. Those girls are almost always sent home because they're not focusing on their own individual relationships (work successes) but instead on what others are doing wrong.

If Justin is a truly shitty employee, his boss will come to realize that on his own and will appreciate Ted just stepping up and doing what needs to be done instead of wasting time figuring out who's not pulling their weight. If and when Ted's boss realizes this and asks him about how Justin is as a manager, he can feel free to express his frustrations. Make sure he does this in a calm, logical manner as no one takes an angry, hysterical person seriously.

Finally, make sure your boyfriend takes you to a fancy AF dinner to thank you for solving his work problems.

Sincerely,
Betches

5.
PLEASE SEE ATTACHED

Advancing in Your Job

Now that we've talked about getting a job and the basic dynamics of office life, it's time to talk about how to actually be *good* at your job, instead of just getting by. We know, it's annoying to constantly have to be on top of your behavior and make improvements. The key to not becoming overwhelmed or burned out by this constant need for improvement is a change in mindset about why you're doing it.

We've found that the best mindset to adopt to help you get through the unpleasant aspects of working is to think about everything you're doing as a bigger project and that project is yourself. We'll admit, the truth is that nothing you're doing at work is *that* important in the long run (unless you're like, a CIA agent or a heart surgeon, and if so, how do you even have time to be reading this?), but the small things you choose to do well or not every day mold who you are as an employee and a person. Your goal should not just be to get through the next draft of your PowerPoint presentation unscathed. Your underlying goal should be to make yourself as good at your job as possible, and if you successfully make that change in yourself and your attitude, perfect PowerPoints will naturally follow. So yes, you might be designing a really boring deck about a product you would never use, but if you reframe it in your mind as working hard for the sake of investing in your own improvement, everything you do suddenly feels a lot more worthy of your efforts.

For this chapter we drew on a lot of our experiences as bosses to give our best advice for how to improve, but remember, you should be trying to make these improvements for your own sake, not to temporarily impress your boss. Be selfish, it works.

MEETINGS: HOW TO NOT BE *THAT* GIRL

For most people who work in a typical office environment, meetings are pretty much the ~~backbone of your schedule~~ bane of your existence. Yes, we would all rather be passing the hours at our desks switching through browser tabs and accumulating Ebates refunds, but the unfortunate reality is that we probably spend about the same amount of time in meetings as we do bingeing Netflix (a statistic we completely made up). The universal feeling about meetings—from intern up to CEO—is pretty much dread. A little part of your soul dies every time you receive a calendar invite.

What makes meetings suck so much? It's probably the fact that you're forced to directly interact with the people you already peripherally interact with the entire day anyway. Add a specific time frame, an agenda to get through, and no way of excusing yourself from the conversation until it's officially over, and you've reached a new level of hell. Not only that, but meetings are a place that you typically have to be on your game. Unless you want to suck at meetings, which is fine, but trust us, everyone notices.

As with everything, we have some tips, mostly based on our experiences in a lot of really shitty meetings.

Know your place: Based on your job title and what the meeting's purpose is, intuit what your role should be. That goes for everybody, from the person running the meeting to the intern "taking minutes" in the corner. There's nothing more annoying than the person who calls a meeting, has no purpose and no goals, and expects everyone to just sit there and do the work for them with no guidance. Same goes for the opposite extreme, the intern who thinks anyone wants to hear her seventy-five opinions. Not that interns' ideas can't be good, it's just that literally no one except Cardi B has seventy-five really great things to say in the span of an hour, so there's no reason for anyone to be interjecting that much.

> *Sit down, lil bitch, be humble.*
> —Kendrick Lamar, probably talking to his interns

Don't talk unless you know what you're talking about: It's not really that hard to follow this piece of advice. If you're not absolutely sure of what you're saying, simply don't waste everyone's time by saying things just for the sake of deluding yourself into thinking that you're contributing.

Be prepared: Our advice about not speaking if you don't know what you're talking about does not apply to things you're directly responsible for. If you were expected to bring something to the table (literally) at this meeting, whether that's status updates, new ideas, goals, or results, always know what you're responsible for prior to the meeting and leave yourself enough time to prepare those things. Sounds like you have to be really on top of your shit all the time, right? Yeah, it's fucking annoying, but news flash, work is annoying. Try your best to not get overwhelmed, keep it simple and organized. Every day, look at your calendar for the next day, see what meetings you have, and then figure out what you will need to have done. Then go do it, obviously. And don't ramble. Just keep your contribution to a couple of sentences that cover your assigned task. No one likes a rambler, and you're undoing any positive impressions you may have made on everyone by not shutting the fuck up after you made your point. Less is more.

> So you see, the puppy was like industry, in that they were both lost in the woods. And nobody, especially the little boy—"society"—knew where to find them. Except that the puppy was a dog. But the industry, my friends, that was a revolution.
>
> —Billy Madison

Big hint: Not every aspect of every meeting needs your input. If you're not sure what to say, just don't participate in that part of the convo. If you're directly asked a question and you still don't know what to say, you can try to bullshit an answer and risk sounding like Billy Madison, or you can spare us all and just say, "I'm not totally sure of the answer but I'll look it up after the meeting and get back to you."

Don't check your phone: We know, it's basically impossible to leave your phone alone. Unless whatever's on your phone is directly work-related and/or urgent (a.k.a. a legit family emergency and not like, watching your puppy cam), turn your phone facedown next to you or leave it at your desk. If you're meeting with someone for coffee, your phone should probably be in your bag the whole time unless there's a good reason you need it out, like if you're a surgeon on call. You want the person to feel like you're valuing their time, and it's hard to convey "I'm listening" if your body language is saying, "Oh, the Betches put up a new Insta story." People, especially your boss, notice when you even pick up your phone, let alone when they watch you scroll through Instagram—and they can for sure tell when you're popping out a quick work email versus when you're scrolling through social. Everyone you know is at work right now. There's nothing that great on Instagram that can't wait to be lunchtime viewing material. Also, your wedding "emergency" is not an emergency; someone will be able to find more Italian marble to carve into rehearsal dinner tables.

Take notes: No, delusional, you're not going to remember what was discussed here today, stop lying to yourself. Even if you paid attention the whole time, which you probably didn't because you definitely zoned out thinking about what to have for dinner, it's just not possible to remember everything for the next meeting. Best to avoid looking like an idiot when you forget to bring the fifteen ideas you brainstormed for next year's offensive Super Bowl commercial. If you aren't taking your own notes, there's probably a notetaker who circulates notes via yet another annoying email afterward. Don't know who the notetaker is? It's definitely you. *Does anyone have a pen?*

No bathroom breaks: If a meeting is an hour or less, go to the bathroom before or after. Don't leave in the middle. Unless you have a medical condition or are pregnant, you can hold it. You're not a three-month-old puppy.

Don't ask questions you should know the answer to: Questions are a great way to pretend you're heavily invested in the conversation, but before you ask the first thing that pops into your head, silently ask yourself: *Should I already know this?* If you're not sure, really think about it before you ask. Every single unnecessary question, no matter how smartly worded, prolongs the meeting, which should be a good disincentive. Here's a secret: if you ask too many questions that keep everyone in the meeting longer, everyone hates you. Would you rather be hated, or go back to your desk to catch up on your online shopping? Put your questions on hold. Ask your work wife or another friendly coworker right after the meeting; they'll hopefully give you the right answer, probably won't judge, and will thank you for not prolonging the meeting.

Don't overstay your welcome: *It's not over; it still isn't over!*—This should not be a quote that applies to the monthly revenue meeting. This advice goes out to all the people running meetings. End it when it's over. Someone will send an incredibly thrilling recap email later. Same goes for starting the meeting. Long convos about how everyone's weekends were are annoying because (1) no one cares, and (2) we saw it on Insta story.

Follow up: A good way to show your manager that you were paying attention and care about WTF happens next is to follow up regarding any confusion or any ways you can assist in accomplishing the meeting's goal. Maybe they asked you to look into something or just simply posed a question that wasn't necessarily directed at you. You don't even have to email them with an immediate answer, you can just say, "I'm right on top of that, Rose!" It's so simple and makes you look *so* responsible.

GOOD MEETINGS VS BAD MEETINGS: AN ANALYSIS

In a Good Meeting . . .	In a Bad Meeting . . .
Everything starts and ends on time.	Things start ten minutes late; end at the last second possible without getting through the whole agenda, requiring everyone to attend a fucking follow-up meeting.
There is an agenda.	There are a lot of updates on what happened at the *Real Housewives* reunion last night.
Everyone participates in correlation to their role and responsibilities for the meeting.	Everyone competes for the spotlight or avoids taking responsibility for screwups.
Someone takes charge and leads the meeting.	No one is taking charge and everyone is zoning out.
There are drinks and snacks.	You can hear everyone chewing.
Everyone pays attention and leaves their phones facedown on the table or at their desk.	You can practically hear everyone scrolling on Instagram above the sound of no one knowing what's going on.
Everyone leaves clear on what their personal next steps are.	Everyone leaves asking WTF just happened.

WORKING FROM HOME:
EVERYONE KNOWS IT'S A JOKE

One of the greatest blessings (but also curses) of working in the digital era is the idea of remote jobs. Blessing: you rarely ever have to commute. Curse: it can put you at risk of becoming a gross piece of shit who never leaves the house, and also, because everyone knows that you're constantly plugged in, they can constantly make demands of you at the simple click of a send button and derail the wine night you had scheduled for 4:00 p.m. So rude.

Some jobs give you the option of working from home on certain days, while some jobs are fully established as remote gigs and never require your in-person presence. In our opinion, unless you're a working mom it's probably better for your long-term sanity and appearance to have the former, as it gives you some semblance of a reason to act like a real human for at least some portion of your week. I mean, you're already spending hungover Sundays as a swamp person, do you really need five extra days of that? And as much as the idea of never being required to be anywhere sounds amazing, the reality is that unless you make an effort to get out of the house, it can turn you into a subway bum who just happens to live in a doorman building.

Plus, the work-from-home fifteen is even worse than the

freshman fifteen, because you're now further into adulthood and your metabolism can't really sustain the schedule of a hibernating bear. Everyone—including your boss (she does it too)—knows working from home is basically just corporate enabling of a weekday afternoon couch-melt while letting your Netflix run in the background until you pause it for a mandatory conference call and act like you've been diligently working all day. If working from home requires you to be on Skype or video chat at any point, your WFH uniform becomes something like a clothing mullet: business on the top, whatever you wore to sleep last night on the bottom.

So with all this freedom, how is it possible to continue being an actual person? You have the gift of no in-person supervision, which is again a blessing and a curse. While this might have sounded amazing in college and called for a full day of weed-smoking and early happy hour, after a while that starts to indicate less of "carefree college life" or "treating yourself" and more of the beginning of a bottomless pit of like, despair. Which sounds even worse than working in an office, TBH.

On the positive side, working from home is an amazing opportunity to revolve your work around your life, rather than making your life revolve around your work, which is the sad reality of most standard nine-to-five jobs. When you work in an office, there's a lot of time when you're not expected to do anything specific, so you waste that time scrolling through lame engagement photos on Facebook or taking quizzes about which type of Ezekiel bread you are, just to appear like you're doing something on your computer. When you work from home, you don't have to pretend you're doing anything, except for the immediate demands of sporadic calls and such. But no one has to know the mechanics behind when or where you get your work done, and that can free up a lot of your time for naps.

Basically, we think you should take your work-from-home days and act like they're just weekends on which you happen to have no drunken plans. Use the time that you would normally spend commuting and make sure you work out. Make yourself food instead of ordering in. (Yes, that shame you feel when you're on your third delivery of the day is much deserved.) If you have room, set up a designated work area with an actual desk for working so that you can "leave" when you're done and create a physical delineation between work and life. You can even make that space look instagrammable so you can take a cute little bird's-eye shot of your notebook and latte with the hashtag #bosslife. (No, we're joking, never fucking do that.) Go work at a coffee shop instead of on your coffee table. Go do errands to get out of your house and take a walk. Argue with your cable provider to get fees taken off your bill. Take a shower. Wash your hair more than once a week, even if you're not seeing anyone you care about. The world is your oyster, don't waste the privilege of working from home on a slow transition from cute normal person into a huge piece of shit who leaves the house as often as Rob Kardashian did in 2016.

MENTORSHIP: CULTIVATING RELATIONSHIPS FOR YOUR BENEFIT

Mentorship is one of those things that, like love, can't be forced. As much as you might try to kiss someone's ass for personal gain, the benefit of having a mentor lies in what they *choose* to do for you that you can't do yourself. And no one is going to do favors for you if they don't think that it's worth it for them or if they don't genuinely believe in you.

Everybody has somebody higher up to please, and for someone to go out on a limb for you, they need to be extremely confident that doing so won't reflect poorly on them later. This should be pretty obvious to you already when you think about what you would be willing to do for someone else. For example, let's say your friend wants to work at your company and asks you to put in a good word for her or pass along her résumé to the hiring manager. Would you be likely to do this if you know she has a history of getting involved with ill-advised office hookups and flipping out on her bosses before abruptly quitting? Probably not.

As hard as it can be to find someone you truly connect with professionally who also gifts you their extra time (no one actually has extra time, so they're basically giving you their free time, which is a really high bar), having a mentor in your career network can be insanely beneficial. We know, it's annoying to get to know new people, but you only need one, maybe two, at any given stage of your career.

Why even get a mentor in the first place? After all, you can survive without one. But whether this person is openly pulling for your advancement within the company or they're just someone who you find easy to talk to and ask for advice, it's really important to build *real* relationships at work, both for the benefit of your career and for like, your sanity. Friends on your same level can listen to you bitch about Nancy in marketing, but a mentor can listen to you bitch about Nancy in marketing while simultaneously offering you real advice on how to deal with her from a place of real experience.

Okay, fine, mentors are great. Where do I get one? So, obviously, it's not really possible to just "get" a mentor. Someone with more experience and who's cool enough for you to want as a mentor isn't just going to like you because you have the best *Game of Thrones* theories every Monday. Ninety-nine percent of people you meet will have no chance of being a potential mentor. They might not have the time, they might not connect with you, or they might not see you as worth going to bat for. Mentoring is a relationship that's cultivated over time, and, like your delusional friend's everlasting hookup she calls her boyfriend, just because you call someone your mentor doesn't make them one. The feeling truly has to be mutual. You'll know if someone could be a good potential mentor if you seem to organically connect on a personal level, not just a transactional work-related level. If they seem interested in speaking to you more than they're literally required to (we don't mean in a harassery way), then this might be a worthwhile relationship to pursue.

A lot of companies nowadays are trying to push formal mentorship programs, particularly for women. While the idea is a nice sentiment, it probably only works in cases where the two people who are assigned to each other actually vibe and add to each other's lives. A successful mentorship from one of these programs is like becoming BFF with your random freshman-year roommate. Possible, but not that likely. That said, if your company has a program, it probably can't hurt to sign up for it just in case.

And you should be wary about who you trust, too. Don't be so desperate for a mentor that you overshare without determining their loyalties first (talk about *Game of Thrones* theories). We've heard countless stories about how older female bosses or "mentors" will play really nice in the beginning and then undercut the younger woman because they feel threatened by a millennial mindset and their ability to potentially replace them. *It's not our fault we actually know how to use hashtags!* We get it, established women worked hard to get where they are, and younger women are constantly displacing older ones in every form of societal cultural expression. So expect some jealousy.

Just be careful with trusting anybody too soon, no matter who they are. Being a mentee requires a degree of vulnerability and admitting that you might need help sometimes (gross). Nobody knows everything, not even you, and that's what the mentor is supposed to be for. But the same rules apply in the opposite direction: You can't break their trust and expect to flourish. Don't go repeating the shit your mentor talked about other people to anyone else, even your work wife. After all, she is only your work wife, not your life wife. Don't go telling their personal stories about how they're afraid their husband has a thing for the nanny. Don't brag about how drunk you get together when you go out for drinks or spill the company secrets they shared during a particularly helpful moment.

If you're trustworthy, people will trust you, and that will definitely contribute to your success in a really big way. So look out for an older, more established, cool, trustworthy person in a position of relative power, see if you have a genuine connection, and then don't screw them over. Easy.

SHOW ME THE MONEY:
HOW TO ASK FOR A RAISE

Let's start this little section off with a disclaimer: the three of us have been asked for raises by employees many times, but we've never personally asked for raises (at least not in the traditional sense). We did, however, once run a social media campaign in partnership with a cosmetics brand where we encouraged women to ask for raises, called #SlayYourPay (clever, we know). So basically, we're either the worst or best possible people to be advising on this topic; you decide.

Much has been said about the wage gap and why it exists (most reliably by men's rights activists in the comments section of our Instagram), and while we're not exactly labor economists, we can surmise that asking for more money will make you more likely to get it versus not asking for it. In all seriousness, one of the most surprising things to us about our own employees has been how infrequently they've asked for raises. We assumed, given all the publicity around the equal-pay issue, that we would be getting more raise-asks. I guess your "feminist fact of the day" Insta stories aren't really moving the needle, Jackie.

We get it, asking for a raise is scary. You don't want to come off as entitled or piss off your boss, and you definitely don't want to hear the word *no*. It's super awkward. I mean, your rent is about to go up and you're trying to finally adopt a puppy, and you need this raise to be able to pay for her shots. If the answer is no, you won't be able to adopt the puppy for another six months and who knows if Fluffy will have found a forever home by then. The stakes couldn't be higher.

Which brings us to the golden rule of raises: it's not personal, it's business. This goes for both the asker and the askee. For your employer, giving you a raise is not some kindhearted decision because you're always good for a compliment and you bonded at happy hour last week. A raise is a financial decision by the company tied to your performance, based on if you'll be contributing financially to their business in proportion to the raise they're giving you. End of story. (If this isn't the case, then whichever fashion blogger you've been "project coordinating" for is truly an idiot.)

In light of this knowledge, the way you ask for a raise should never, *ever* be personal. Seriously, don't even think of bringing up Fluffy. We're going to make asking for a raise insanely easy for the rest of your life by telling you the exact argument that we, as bosses, want to hear when you're asking us to pay you more. It's called the Show Me the Money Method and we've made it really easy to remember:

Show: Come prepared to your boss with a concise and persuasive summary of what you've achieved and contributed to the company since you started working there and/or since your last raise;

bonus points if you're able to show how this translates into actual revenue. Even more bonus points if you've typed that shit up and made it pink and scented. Kidding, but the key here is to highlight all the ways that the company has materially and financially benefited and will continue to benefit from having you there, and to emphasize how seriously you take this discussion. Show that the ask is not about you going on more shopping sprees, it's about the financial well-being of the company. Fucking duh.

Me: Talk about your favorite topics: you and your plans for the future. And we don't mean your next PTO. What you're saying to your boss is "This is why you need *me* really badly." Talk about ways you've uniquely gone above and beyond your job description, how you're going to continue to do so, and be specific about the ways you can and will expand your role. The difference between these points and the ones in the SHOW category is SHOW is a recap of your standard job performance, while ME is where you should highlight the things that you weren't asked to do but did anyway and will continue to do going forward. Paint a picture of what results would not have been attained without *your specific* ingenuity and creativity. Always keep the focus on how everything *you* do will all be worth more to the company and that's why they need to reward you. You should subtly be planting the idea in your boss's head that you could always take your talents elsewhere, to one of their competitors even. The key here is subtly showing them why they need to reward and incentivize *you* specifically so you can do amazing things for *them*.

The: *The* is a filler word.

Money: Take your explanation of how much more revenue your expanded role is going to generate in the future and throw out a number you feel your salary should be raised. If you want a raise so your salary is more in line with the market rate in your company's industry, add that in. You should try to pick the highest number that safely keeps you in the range of not being laughed out of the room. You also don't *have* to pick a number, but know that if you don't do so, you're at the mercy of your employer's ~~frugality~~ business savvy and limiting your ability to be all like, *I object!* when they try to raise you too little.

Speaking of negotiating, that's a whole other phase of the conversation, which might extend over multiple conversations. We generally feel that you should always try to negotiate, as it's expected that you would do so. Don't feel like trying to negotiate is disrespectful or out of line, this isn't the marketplace in Thailand where the guy made you feel all guilty about haggling on the price of the thumb-size clay pots that you never even ended up using. The worst anyone can say is no. Again, it's not personal, it's business, and anyone with the power to give you a raise is aware of that and hopefully won't hold it against you. As long as your raise ask is in line with your true contribution as an employee, it's not crazy to ask for more, so be self-aware.

The key to winning any negotiation is having another option, so if you're in a position where you may want to leave your job and are able to do so, then there's no harm in utilizing this other opportunity as leverage for a raise at your current job (if you wouldn't mind staying, of course). Just make sure that you would actually *want* to pursue this other offer (and that the other offer is legitimately real), because you definitely don't want to find yourself in a situation where you used a job offer you didn't really want as a negotiating tactic, and your old employer didn't rise to the occasion, so now you have to take the job you didn't really want. Or now you have no job, if you faked having an offer and then couldn't back down. And if that other offer is going to pay you more and you'd rather do it anyway, then WTF are you still doing asking your current boss for a raise? Don't waste his or her time.

Another common circumstance is that your boss will say yes to a raise but not allow it to go into effect immediately. In that case, you should suggest ways that you could expand your role over the next few months to prove yourself and ask for feedback about your goals and what results they would like to see from you in the meantime. Not every manager is going to have patience for this much hands-on feedback, so obviously you should try to feel out if this is the right way to impress your manager. Other managers might prefer blow jobs under the desk, and you should promptly report them to HR.

Either way, our point is that there is no better time than mid-raise discussion to put in a sincere effort to prove that you are worth the money you're asking for. Just figure out what would make a difference in your position, make a plan, do it, and then show them what you did. The bottom line is that everyone in this discussion is looking for the same thing: money. Make more money for the company, and they will give some of it to you. Unless we're talking about a certain notorious discount store that rhymes with mallmart.

MAKE LIKE THE JEFFERSONS: MOVIN' ON UP

As bosses, we've always believed that promotions should happen naturally and that by the time we promote somebody, they've already basically stepped into that new role. We don't believe in promoting just because "you've been here a year." You're not so much working for the sake of earning a promotion in title (like, yay, good for you, but can you actually do any part of the job better than you could when you started?), but you should always be working hard and getting better at your job, so you'll sort of earn the promotion automatically. No company is ever going to promote somebody before it's deserved and then just cross their fingers that the employee proves their hope well-founded.

So how do you actually earn a promotion? Here's what would make us want to promote someone:

They can fill a new need that the company didn't have before. Sometimes the need for a new role will come up where it didn't exist before. This could happen because the industry has evolved and now the company needs someone to do that job full-time. Maybe the company wasn't even going to necessarily go in a certain direction but someone started working on a certain project or tasks, and now they created a new revenue opportunity in this area, so they got promoted into that job. For example, someone on staff who made an established company like Nike a website in the nineties would probably be super valuable and likely got promoted.

They've done a really good job and have grown into a higher title within their department. For example, being promoted to marketing director from assistant marketing director. Maybe we had to hire someone under you, maybe it's just a title promotion because you've substantially grown within your job and gotten some really good results, maybe you're solid overall and have been there long enough and it's clear to everyone you deserve a promotion.

If you're all like, *Betches, that is way too vague, give us some concrete examples,* here is our guide to what type of things would or wouldn't earn you a promotion at Betches Media.

We would promote someone who:	We probs wouldn't promote someone who:
Foresees what we will ask them to do and does it before they're asked.	Online shops while waiting to be told what to do.
Always thinks of new ways to do a better job.	Always thinks of new ways to get out of doing something.
Doesn't dip out at exactly 5:00 p.m. every single day.	Leaves at 4:45; claims to work from home the rest of the night but Insta stories from happy hour.
Doesn't abuse the unlimited vacation policy.	Acts like every third Friday of the month is a bank holiday.
Generally gets along with everyone.	Sends passive-aggressive Slack messages about the sales team.
Pays attention to detail and doesn't make careless mistakes.	Can't get a lunch order right.
Takes feedback well and tries to improve.	Has more excuses for mistakes than the fuckboy you met while day drinking.

Basically, if you want a promotion, you have to work for it. And that's okay, because people generally value things they put effort into getting. (Just ask a guy who you waited to have sex with.) It's worthwhile to be promoted to a position with more responsibilities and a higher salary if you're at a company you like and they treat you well, and you don't have any immediate plans or desire to leave. But just being blasé about your performance isn't going to be as worthwhile of an experience than it will be if you try, especially not if you're trying to get promoted or get a raise. Like with everything else, it's not personal, it's business. Unless the boss is your dad.

ARE YOU MANAGEMENT MATERIAL?

One of the things to consider while aspiring to a promotion is what that promotion will actually entail. It's not just doing what you're doing while getting paid more for it; surprise, your boss will actually expect that you take on more responsibilities and deliver more. Ugh. The truth is that with a promotion often comes managing other people, which is an entirely different skill set than just doing your job at a more advanced level, and it's not meant for everyone.

Based on our experience of hiring and managing people, we've created a checklist to help you understand if you would actually be good at and enjoy managing people. If you don't check off at least six out of these ten items, you might not be the world's best boss.

_____ I'm good at assigning tasks to other people (communicating the goals, explaining directions) with a deadline, and then stepping back and letting them do the tasks without harassing and trying to control them constantly.

_____ I prefer coming up with and executing big ideas rather than small concepts and details.

_____ I take responsibility for my successes and failures and don't try to blame other people for my results.

_____ I have patience for explaining things more than once.

_____ I don't mind listening to people who complain and expect me to help them solve their problems.

_____ I am highly organized and can anticipate what needs to be done ahead of time.

_____ I want more responsibility than I already have.

_____ I'm okay with babysitting adult(s).

_____ I'm good with making budgets and sticking to them.

_____ I'm good at giving feedback and constructive criticism without flipping the fuck out.

TRANSITIONING INTO MANAGEMENT:
FAKE IT TILL YOU MAKE IT

Congrats on your new promotion! Now it's time for the annoying part: the actual promotion. One of the hardest transitions
you'll probably make in a successful career is the first time you
become someone's boss. In our case, because we knew what
a huge responsibility it would be, we delayed hiring any full-
time employees until we were positive that we could make the
commitment and take on the responsibility of actually being
in charge of people. Unless you're Sonja Morgan and think it
flies to hold some college students hostage in your brownstone
while calling them your "interns," the process of becoming
someone's boss is a pretty serious step. Whether this means
hiring people for your own company or getting your first direct
report, it's not as easy as it looks. Suddenly "I don't know" is
no longer an acceptable answer to certain questions, as you're
now the person who is supposed to "know." You're not only
responsible for yourself but also for the people who you're supposed to be managing, and "they're annoying as fuck" isn't
an appropriate comment when doing someone's yearly eval or
when deciding why not to give them a raise.

This is the time to step into the bigger role, and no matter
how prepared you are or how much you deserve it, it's going
to be a challenge. Chances are if you earned a promotion,

you're more than capable of executing the tasks required or else you wouldn't have been promoted in the first place, and it helps to remind yourself of that reality when you're feeling unsure. The biggest challenges will likely come in figuring out the nuances of the new position, realizing that you're in a greater position of power and responsibility, and adjusting yourself and your mindset to what that entails. As always, let's compare this to dating. Think of your entry-level, non-management job as being the guy you're hooking up with. It's nice, the stakes are low, you can come and go as you please (after 5:00 p.m.) without feeling that committed. Now think of getting promoted to manager as being in a relationship. You're seriously accountable to the job, and you're going to have to make sacrifices a lot more frequently. Think of the LinkedIn announcement of your new title as your first couple's Instagram. Like a relationship, a promotion is something really exciting and rewarding that most people want, but making it successful in the long term actually takes work and requires a change in how you view yourself (a.k.a. not single) and how you act.

The best advice we can really offer when dipping your toe into the management pool is to fake it till you make it. You've never done this before, so guess what, you have no idea what the fuck you're doing. And that's okay. No one is born knowing how to be a manager, and you're going to make mistakes and feel like an idiot sometimes, so be prepared for that and accept it. This is when it's really helpful to have a mentor, or at least a friend who is already a manager, so you can ask their advice. Even with help, it's going to take practice and communication with whomever you're managing. Maybe try to pick a boss whose style you thought was good, and try to emulate them in some ways. Ask yourself what you think they would do in a situation you're not sure about. Also try not to stress too much and worry too much about what people are thinking; *you're* the boss, and therefore people sort of automatically assume that you know what you're doing until you show them otherwise.

So just act like it's fine and you have a handle on what's going on (unless you are completely desperate and in over your head in crisis mode, then fucking ask someone). If you don't know the basics of what's going on, now would probably be a good time to try to figure it out while not inspiring panic in your underlings. Keep your freak-outs low-key, hopefully in your brand-new private office. Seriously, just relax. Remember that things probably just *feel* like a bigger deal than they are because it's a new experience, but every successful person you look up to had their first days of being managers, and they probably felt just as insecure as you do. It's fine, just go meditate or something.

NOW I'M THE BOSS: HOW DO I DO IT?

We're sure everybody thinks when they get promoted that they're going to be the most amazing boss ever. You've learned from the terrible things that were done to you, and there's just *no way* you would be such a dick to the people who work for you. What's the big deal if there's an extra zero in one spreadsheet cell? No one died, so you're *definitely* not going to torture anyone over it, right? *Right?!*

Wrong.

The first thing you learn when you're in charge is that it's not the endless power trip it appeared to be when you were in the lower position. Your boss wasn't getting mad at you because they enjoyed being mad (unless they are a sociopath and then, yes, they were). The secret is that *everybody* has someone or something to answer to. Your boss has a boss, and if he or she is pissed off at you, it's probably just because they're scared of how your results will affect them. Even Warren Buffett has to answer to his shareholders, his own portfolio, and his grandkids who are probably all like, *WTF is Grandpa doing with our trust fund?! Giving it to poor people and the arts again?!* And when you're at the top, you might even learn that your biggest critic is actually yourself, which is not necessarily a better internal feeling than when someone else is telling you to work twelve-hour days.

As managers ourselves, we've realized that it's extremely easy to be judged as harsh or overly critical, when all you're expecting is that tasks be completed competently and with a positive attitude, while not needing to hold your employees hands throughout the process. If that is a mostly accurate description of you at work, you're probably considered a good employee.

Remember when *The Devil Wears Prada* came out and everyone thought Miranda Priestly was some sort of monster and Anna Wintour thought it was a PR disaster? We actually think the opposite: Miranda was the victim of that movie. Think about it, she gives her assistant a paycheck and the opportunity to work in what was widely regarded as a "dream job" that would enable her to work "anywhere" after one year, and yet somehow Meryl Streep's character is the villain because she expects Andy to hand her a turquoise belt while simultaneously keeping her opinions to herself? Seriously, other than the *Harry Potter* thing, what was so hard about Andy's job? Making a reservation at Pastis? Hanging up ten to fifteen skirts from Calvin Klein? If you can't figure out how to deliver the book without being derailed by two eight-year-old

> Details of your incompetence do not interest me.
>
> —Miranda Priestly,
> *The Devil Wears Prada*

gingers, then maybe you don't deserve to go to Paris, and not just because you eat carbs.

Because this movie was based on a book, inspired by a real person and magazine, it's a really amazing example of how a strong female boss with high expectations is unfairly vilified (whereas Harvey Weinstein's overall shitty behavior was only brought to light publicly because he also happened to allegedly be breaking the law as a rapist, but TBH, he probably could've continued throwing staplers at assistants' heads without consequences if not for that other thing). *Vogue* didn't become *Vogue* because "small" mistakes were accepted and positively reinforced. You may think it's stupid or unimportant to make sure you bring your boss her coffee the way she wants it, but if anyone thought you could handle more seemingly important tasks right now, you would already be doing them. Getting your boss a coffee is not about her being a diva or creating busywork to fill your time; she asked you to do it so she could be enabled to take care of higher-level tasks without wasting time in the Starbucks line.

If your boss was spending time running her own errands, that would hinder her ability to concentrate on moving the business forward in bigger ways and you could potentially get laid off. Similarly, the consequences are much bigger if she fucks up. If the boss screws up badly enough, a whole brand or company can go down with them.

So it doesn't matter that *Vogue* doesn't cure cancer or end poverty, the point is that when you work anywhere, the company that's writing your paychecks is entitled to expect that you do your job well and leave your shitty attitude at the security desk. You were hired to be part of a team that accomplishes a goal, and you should try to take pride in the part you play rather than demeaning the importance of your own tasks. That's the lesson that Nigel was trying to teach Andy when she came whining to him about Miranda. Judging your boss for "flipping out over small details" is immature and shows that you don't understand the bigger picture of how to grow into a successful career. Keep that bad attitude up and you'll never earn the privilege of flipping out at your assistant for bringing your cappuccino with whole milk instead of almond.

Let's be clear, we're in no way advocating being emotionally abusive or mean for no reason just because you have people working under you. We would never recommend trying to be anything less than respectful, patient, and thoughtful with the people you manage. But you also shouldn't worry that you're expecting too much and therefore lower your expectations for the sake of seeming nice. That's the kind of shit that keeps the glass ceiling intact, because women's fear of coming off as "mean" causes them to do a mediocre job. The way to "be nice" is to ask for what you need politely, with as reasonable a deadline as you can give, and be open and available to answer questions and give feedback. The answer is not to assign fewer tasks or accept shittier work so your employees don't feel sad.

While we can't map out how to handle every single situation, there are a few common threads of the types of annoying things employees or direct reports do and our advice for handling them.

The one who demands too much of your time: This is probably the most consistently annoying type of employee, but the important thing to remember about this person is that she is simply an attention-starved human being, so it has very little to actually do with you. As a manager, it's not your job to babysit this person. It's one thing to answer questions to avoid mistakes or for the sake of thoroughness; it's another when your employee needs to schedule multiple sit-downs during his or her first week to figure out how to set up their new email account. Your boss is not your fucking Sherpa guiding you up the treacherous mountain of submitting your onboarding documents to HR. *Ask. Someone. Else.*

You should always respond to real, legitimate questions (the ones that are your job to answer) with real, legitimate answers. Even if this person is constantly annoying you with questions, it's likely that giving real answers to good questions will help the person complete their tasks and help them learn in the long term, which will ultimately benefit you. The key is learning to discern which questions are just cries for attention, and—when those questions arise—basically tell them to figure it the fuck out. You should not begin a pattern of reinforcing annoying question-asking and time-seeking behavior, because once you do, they will never learn to do anything themselves and you will find yourself constantly pissed off at them. You will only enable their addiction to your attention and approval, and they will never improve.

However, if you're able to train them to distinguish between a legitimate, worth-your-while question and the matters for which they need to put in like, ten extra seconds of thought, there's actually a chance that they can stop seeking attention. The way to do that is by giving them the attention they want when it's reasonable and constructive, and not giving them that desired attention when it's not.

When you sense a question that's a waste of your time, don't be mean about it, because attention-seekers love negative attention just as much as positive. Refer them to someone else on the team or tell them to google it, just keep the time interacting with them as short as possible so they get the picture through your actions. Do this again and again over time, and they will reduce their attention-whoring ways or at least focus them on someone else, hopefully a therapist. They will have you to thank for that, and their future bosses can thank you, too. It's basically like a corporate pay-it-forward program.

The one who does the bare minimum: If you're doing the bare minimum, you're already doing less than the bare minimum. When have you ever heard someone describing even a mediocre employee as someone who can always be counted on to do the bare minimum? We get it—it's easy to understand why people would enter a job, especially a first job, thinking this is okay. Simple reason: this tactic worked in college. Honestly, if there's one thing the American school system really screwed up on, it's reinforcing bare-minimum behavior by making school all about numbers and grades, rather than about effort and execution of ideas. There's no grade for working really hard but failing; an F is just an F and it connotes the same value as the work of someone who didn't even try and also failed, which is a really bad life lesson. If your goal, especially if the task is something you don't like doing, is to just try to pass, then as long as you can do that, it doesn't really matter what the exact output is. It's a pretty big shock to some people who arrive on day one of their first job expecting to complete their to-do list by noon and spend the rest of the day tagging their friends in memes, when they find that this expectation will screw you over and that most work days are not going to be "chill," even at your dream job.

A common move we've noticed people will pull when they are either too lazy to do something, or don't like the task they've been assigned, is that they will claim to be "confused" about what they're supposed to do. Or they'll do something poorly and then blame their shitty work on being confused or "not having enough clarification." This is probably one of our biggest pet peeves as managers, because it's the employee's way of subtly blaming their boss for the shitty job they did, and gaslighting them into believing they are bad at explaining things. As an employee, if you don't understand something, fucking think about it for ten seconds before claiming you're confused, or before blaming your shitty work on your confusion. Unless your boss gave you instructions in ancient Greek, being confused is only one person's fault: your own.

On the bright side, as a manager, an employee who does the bare minimum is probably one of the easier things to fix through positive reinforcement and feedback. It's pretty simple: whenever someone does something that's not good enough, just make them do it again until it is. You're probably going to have to reject what they do many times until they get the picture, and you might be questioning if you're too critical, but don't cave and let them off the hook until you're legitimately happy with the result. That is literally the only way their work will get better. You can try to speed up this process by showing them what good work looks like, and every time they improve even a little bit without your direct help, praise them with positive feedback. Be specific about what you liked and what you didn't like. Show increasing disapproval over repetition of the same mistakes you already corrected multiple times. Don't be a bitch when something is bad, but don't baby them, tell them it's okay, and then fix it for them. Stick to your guns.

Think about it, if you're training your puppy to sit and every time he doesn't listen to you you give him a treat and then sit down yourself, your dog will end up fat and disobedient. We're not comparing employees to dogs (okay, fine, we kind of are, but that could honestly be considered a compliment in some circles), we're just saying don't do people's work for them, because it will only teach them to continue doing a lackluster job and wasting your time.

The one who picks and chooses their tasks: Slightly less bad than the person who does the bare minimum is the one who picks and chooses what work they want to do and does a shitty job with the rest. Even good jobs have a fair amount of strings attached, and it's literally impossible to find a job where every single task you're doing is enjoyable. That pleasure is reserved for vacation, sleep, or a day in the life of Kate Moss.

The employee who picks and chooses their tasks is someone who does a pretty good or very good job with the things they like to do and then either drops the ball completely, ignores, or does a half-assed job with the things they don't like. They're somehow simultaneously amazing and awful to have working for you, and there are a few different ways you can approach this type of flaw.

First, you can always just fire them. That option is nice to have in the back of your head at all times, but realistically it's not the best idea, because hiring and training new people is extremely annoying and time-consuming, and this person is already pretty good at their job in some ways. There's no guarantee that a new person would be better, and then you've put all this effort into firing, hiring, and retraining someone just to maybe end up with equal or worse results. It's like dating a guy about whom you love everything, except he leaves his clothes on the floor and his dishes in the sink. Are you going to break up with an otherwise perfect guy just because he clearly grew up with a mother who cleaned up after him constantly? Maybe, but if you really love him, you'll figure out a solution.

Second, you can try to shift their assigned work tasks so

that they're doing more of what they're very good at and don't have to do as much of what they're not good at. This strategy might seem efficient, but it doesn't always work if you don't have the right person to cover the other tasks; plus you're subtly reinforcing the person's bad attitude toward half their job and teaching them that they don't have to do anything they don't want to. So shifting their work doesn't really fix the underlying problem.

A final option, and the best one, is to give them feedback during which you explain that their approach is not acceptable and then basically just withhold a promotion or a raise until they change this pattern. They're clearly capable; they just need to put in more effort on the tasks they don't care for. Have an honest conversation and make it clear to them that you expect them to do just as good a job at answering customer service emails as they do with brainstorming ironic happy hour themes. Figure out what motivates them and then frame it in those terms. For example, if you know their secret dream is to become a *Bachelorette* contestant, ask them if they would ever submit their application with a video as poorly done as the Instagram story they just created. This method definitely requires a lot more care, effort, and consistency on your part than the others, and it'll probably take time to see a change while this person reforms their lifelong avoidance instincts. But if done effectively, you might end up with a really good employee who goes above and beyond with everything. This will reflect well on you, making it truly worth the effort you put into dealing with them.

The one who causes drama: This person is somehow under the impression that they work at some sort of off-campus Kappa annex. Some examples of drama would be talking a more-than-average amount of shit about coworkers, complaining constantly, making inappropriate comments in meetings, spreading rumors and gossip—i.e., all the things that make work fun and get you through the day. Trust us, we know it's way more fun to rage-text your coworker about how much you hate Janie from sales than it is to edit the same pitch deck for the thousandth time, and it's to be expected that every office has a certain level of drama. Unless you work in one of those offices that has meditation rooms and positivity pods, there's probably no one who cares enough to spend time policing your run-of-the-mill shit-talking.

However, there is a line, and as a manager, it's necessary to figure out where that line is in order to avoid becoming the eye of the office storm. In our opinion, the line is crossed when office politics takes up more than 10 percent of anyone's mental energy and time. Any more than this, and that person is probably toxic. Maybe this person just has a really negative and immature attitude toward work but gets along with everyone, or is rude to the coworkers everyone already hates. As much as we secretly love drama when it happens at our friend's bachelorette party, if you want to actually embody your leadership position, you should avoid personal conflict like the plague and distance yourself from drama.

These people waste theirs and others' time, they make their coworkers feel bad and paranoid, and they cause rifts in the team, which makes everyone less productive and more miserable over time. The challenge is that they usually have amazing gossip that you're dying to hear or they did something extremely scandalous, which everyone naturally gravitates toward because work is boring and gossip provides excitement. Even being the boss doesn't make you immune to the adrenaline rush of hearing that Brittany backhandedly called Sharon fat during the monthly team breakfast. *God, Brittany, you can't just ask people why they're eating white bread!*

So now that you're in charge, how do you deal with them as the boss? The first habit that you need to kick when you get promoted and are now someone else's boss is your own ever-present desire to gossip and talk about office drama. This is because when you do that, you're sending the message that it's okay, which will obviously make that behavior more prevalent. Even if you yourself are a notorious office gossip, it's time to curb it. If you want other people to stop doing it, then you have to stop yourself. If someone wants to talk to you about someone else, politely acknowledge it and try to change the subject or pretend you're busy rather than being all like, *Tell me everything.*

We're not saying this is easy. Sometimes office gossip is the only excitement you have in the seemingly endless work-week, like a cigarette break that will never give you a black lung, only a black heart.

Let's say your assistant made the happy hour reservation at the wrong location. Let's say she does it all the time, and you're at the end of your rope. Text that shit to your boyfriend, call your mom and bitch to her, but don't talk to your co-workers about it in a gossipy fashion. In general, you should do everything in your power to tame, not encourage, office drama. This isn't even necessarily about being a good person or a good boss, it's also about self-preservation; because in a high-drama environment, it's only a matter of time before you will find yourself as the subject of it. Being fodder for gossip is one of those annoying things that comes with being the boss, like suddenly being the one responsible for making sure your department doesn't abuse the lunch stipend. Totally not the person you want to be, but it's just the less exciting flipside of not having to get your time off approved and getting your own office. With great power comes great responsibility to keep your opinions to yourself, even though everyone knows Rachel is a total fucking moron and the only thing she can do consistently is get your Seamless order wrong every single day.

The one who literally just sucks: If they suck at their job, can't seem to be trained, and add nothing positive to the situation, just fire them. And don't let any sexual or discriminatory comments hit them on the way out.

YOUR EMPLOYEE LITERALLY JUST SUCKS: HOW TO FIRE THEM WITHOUT GETTING SUED

Ugh, firing. Seems not that bad; is actually terrible. The act of firing someone is not the hard part; it's really the ramp-up and deciding if it's worth it, and then setting the situation up to be legal and not inconvenience yourself too much. Sometimes you'll get to decide slowly whether you want to fire someone (a slow burn), but sometimes they'll commit some sort of serious indiscretion and you have to do it immediately (let's call it a bonfire). Let's examine both scenarios.

For a slow burn, you've known for a while that someone totally sucks at their job, but there isn't one specific indiscretion you would point to as the reason for firing them. In this case, you should document over time the ways in which they're falling short and keep a record of the negative feedback you gave them over time to document your case that they aren't cutting it. This is to legally protect yourself from potentially getting sued for a discriminatory fire or something like that. At the same time, you should be making a plan for who's going to cover their shit when they leave and try to find someone else so you have an immediate replacement and don't have to waste time recruiting without someone in the role.

For a bonfire, you probably have some sort of situation where the thing the employee did was so obviously egregious that you had to get rid of them immediately. Think legal issues, financial crimes, sexual harassment. You won't be able to recruit in advance, and that will suck, but you definitely shouldn't keep someone around after they've seriously fucked up because you're too lazy to recruit. That could result in even more problems and potentially some really bad PR for the company.

In both cases, the ideal way to fire is quickly and easily. You send them a calendar invite with a vague title to be held in a private place at the end of the day, ideally with a witness from HR to corroborate the conversation. You say, "We're sorry, but we're going in a different direction and we have to let you go." That's it, don't fill in the awkward silence with more words or apologies. If they ask why, want feedback, or beg for their job, you can say that, no, they can't have their job, but you will consult your attorney and see if you're allowed to give them feedback. The goal is to say as little as possible so that you don't land yourself in a precarious legal situation. Give them their severance agreement, and if they try to negotiate, pull the need-to-talk-to-legal response so you don't have to answer on the spot. Ask them to hand in their company property immediately, and have someone else in the office (probably HR) remove them from Slack and email, and cancel their credit cards. No one needs to deal with credit card revenge from your newly fired nonemployee. And change the passwords of all accounts they're on; you don't need them fucking up your entire gorgeous Instagram grid because they're pissed at you, or worse, changing the password on *you*.

The goal with a firing is to make it as quick, painless, and legal as possible for everyone involved. We'd be lying if we said it's easy, and we're not even the ones getting fired.

TL;DR

So like, hopefully this long-ass chapter covered everything you ever wanted to know about office life. Now you can go to work armed with the knowledge of what you're doing wrong, what you should be doing instead, and how to deal with the shit you usually just spend your day complaining about via Slack. Now all you have to do is just like, go do it. K bye.

Dear Betches,

Recently at work EVERYONE in my group has decided to confide in me about their personal problems. My college friends joke with me that I'm a terrible listener so I'm not sure what about me suddenly looks approachable or good at giving advice—maybe it's because my cubicle is the only one with a door, so it acts as a free therapist's office, IDK.

I have become the go-to person about boyfriend problems, which coworkers hate each other, incestuous office hookups, yeast infections, etc. Don't get me wrong, I love a little juicy gossip, but with coworkers I feel like it's really easy to become inappropriate quickly, especially when the drama concerns other coworkers. I don't know if it's appropriate to mention the dilemma to my boss without sounding unprofessional myself.

Additionally, I recently got a promotion (got inspiration from "How to Slay Your Pay"!) with a much greater workload, so I'm honestly just trying to get my work done so I can go home on time to binge-watch *Friends*. I don't want to put myself in a position where it sounds like I'm talking shit about everyone even though I literally pretend to be deaf when I hear someone come in my office. I like maintaining casual relationships with them all and doing fun things after work like happy hours, etc., but it's getting to a point where even that is uncomfortable. Is it possible to be casual friends with coworkers while also keeping boundaries in the relationship and maintaining some sense of professionalism?

Sincerely,
Betch Who Feels Like Jorge the Bartender from
Bachelor in Paradise

Dear Jorge,

It seems unlikely that you've gotten the reputation as the office therapist out of nowhere. While this may annoy you now, it's pretty safe to assume that there was a time when you were not only fielding your coworkers' office drama but giving off the impression that you loved hearing about it and were down to gossip with them.

We don't blame you, betches love talking shit, and we love drama that doesn't have to do with us even more. It can make a workday way more exciting and distract us from the drudgery of office life. Getting involved in a little office excitement now and then isn't the worst thing that can happen, but it seems like you've been indulging so frequently that it's getting in the way of your productivity and potentially your ability to be taken seriously at work.

The solution here is pretty simple. It's all about being honest while also seeming chill. The next time a cubicle mate comes to you with a scandalous story about Jake in accounting, tell her that while you love gossip as much as the next girl, you have a shit ton of work to do and can't focus on it at the moment. Make like, a sad face, but be firm. Let her know that if she wants to talk about something that bothers her, she can call you outside of work hours or should maybe run her dilemma by someone who's a little more objective and doesn't work in your office. You can also mention that knowing so much private stuff about your coworkers makes it hard for you to be professional with everyone and makes things awkward for you sometimes. Everyone appreciates honesty much more than they appreciate being told on, so definitely take this first step to handle it yourself before you get any supervisors involved. Even though it's uncomfortable to say this to someone who's trying to confide in you, it will ultimately make you more trustworthy to all parties involved because that person probably won't assume that you're going to go talk shit about them to someone else now.

Make it clear to your coworkers that you're not in HR and you're simply trying to do the same thing they're there to do: get all your shit done so you can go home and zone out watching Netflix. If you say this enough, your office mates should get the memo and you'll look even more legit to the people around you.

Sometimes maximizing your productivity is about setting boundaries even if you honestly really do kind of want to know which of your coworkers contracted an STI from the office fuckboy.

Sometimes you've got to be a little cruel to be kind.

Sincerely,

Betches

6.
ALL THE BEST

Starting Your Own Company

The majority of this book focuses on navigating the workplace as a person who isn't their own boss and assumes they don't want to be. It's perfectly okay to be someone who doesn't want to start her own thing. It's hard, time-consuming, stressful, and does not offer immediate security (and don't let any of those "empowering" inspirational interviews with successful female entrepreneurs in *Fast Company* fool you into thinking otherwise). Trust us, we're doing it right now. It's kind of like dating a noncommittal douchebag, even if no one would ever dare say it in their 30 Under 30 quote. So then why do so many people go out on their own?

If we wanted to lie, we'd say we started Betches because we've always had "entrepreneurial spirits" and were interested in the way the business world works. False. We started Betches anonymously, not because of some high-level business strategy but because we wanted to get jobs after graduating college and knew that writing honestly about binge drinking and sorority rush was not exactly going to send the message "I'm highly responsible and aspire to a high-powered career."

We started the original blog because we thought we were funny. We paid for a WordPress site and called it betcheslovethis.com. No joke, we had a twenty-minute discussion about whether it was worth it to spend the extra eight dollars to get rid of the .wordpress in the URL because we thought it might just be some stupid project we spent only one night on (Jordana ended up putting it on her credit card, and then Sami and Aleen paid her back via the cable bill). We didn't have a plan, we just felt that no one was writing what we wanted to be reading. There were a lot of people writing funnyish things at the time but not in a way that truly spoke to our perspective. We felt that there was always something lacking from the content that was being targeted to us as millennial women, and once Betches went viral, we thought, *Why* can't *we just do it ourselves?* So we did.

After Betches started to pick up, the word *monetization* didn't come out of our mouths for at least a year. We literally didn't know what the term meant. Business in general was foreign to us. Like how-to-use-Excel foreign. And like any true artistes, we took ourselves so seriously that we thought having advertisers would dilute our content and make it "dishonest." We had something of a "Will circle back later, Susan" type of relationship with business. Literally no fucking clue. We were waking up late (and by late we mean like, well into the p.m. hours) and enjoying our lives and weren't too focused on what would come next.

But when it came to making super-funny, relatable content (and content for us at the time meant writing blog posts), we just knew exactly what to do. The skills felt like our sweet spot. We knew what was gold and what sucked. And while we may not have been focused on making money, we were insanely focused on making the writing perfect and would literally slave over finding the perfect words for what we wanted to say and make jokes about. The work clicked, and we were confident that this project was what we were good at, so we ran with it.

We've been around for seven years, but it wasn't until we were four years into this business that we legitimately decided to proactively monetize our content. In all honesty, we're still figuring it out. Yes, we were making enough money to fund our own lives, but nowhere near enough to fund a full-fledged business with employees, an office, and a marketing budget. The first four years were about investing our time into building our brand and organically growing the audience through content output.

Hahaha. That last sentence is literally a bunch of bullshit

buzzwords that we can confidently say in retrospect, but if you had asked us in 2013 to succinctly define what we were doing we'd say, "We write funny shit; leave us alone."

We're going to let you in on a little but like, monumental secret: no one actually knows what the fuck they're doing. They really don't, not 100 percent. Everyone who's launched a business knows a limited amount, and then the rest of the time they guess, ask a mentor/adviser/investor, google it, or make shit up. Or they're delusional and think they have it all figured out, but if that were true, there would be a lot fewer failed businesses.

And on top of that, nothing is as easy or glamorous as it looks on Instagram. Like those fucking checklists and bullet journals, or pics of a computer screen and a matcha latte, those aren't real life. In reality, the person who posted that just spent thirty minutes cleaning her finger oil from her track pad and twirling her fucking milk foam design to get the perfect picture. Does that sound

> **Romy:** *Do you have some sort of businesswoman special?*
>
> **Truck Stop Waitress:** *Come again?*
>
> **Romy:** *Well, we're businesswomen.*
>
> **Michele:** *Yeah, from LA.*
>
> **Romy:** *And you know how some places have like, a lunch special?*
>
> **Michele:** *For business-women . . .*
>
> **Truck Stop Waitress:** *We don't have anything like that.*
>
> —Romy and Michele's High School Reunion

like something that moves the needle on a profitable business to you?

Successful people, i.e., those who make their own money, not simply activate a trust fund or ask their dads for "a small business loan," struggle to get where they are. They sacrifice a lot and don't make any money in the beginning. Some take second mortgages out on their homes to keep their business afloat, others live with their parents to save money, and some people don't even have that privilege. All are pretty fucking brutal. We lived with our parents after college, we'd know.

The reason we're telling you this is that so many people feel deterred from committing to what they want to do because they see what's already out there and don't feel like there's a space for them. But you should never compare yourself to other people.

DO: Look to others for inspiration and advice.

DON'T: Sit on the couch scrolling through Instagram feeling defeated because everyone looks like they know what they're doing and you don't, therefore you just shouldn't try.

If you start to compare yourself to others, just slap yourself in the face and say: *Stop it, bitch! Go do it*. Turn off *Vanderpump Rules*—James Kennedy will still be a drunk mess when you turn it back on later—and start planning your future.

So why should you listen to us after we just admitted to spending upwards of three years fucking around before we truly started concentrating on growing our business financially? Well, first of all, fun fact: most businesses operate at a loss, and even some of the big-name millennial pink–branded companies that you would probably aspire to build yourself are pretty much just spending their investors' capital in the hope of becoming profitable later on. (Fun fact: we've never taken outside investment. We've taken some loans but we fund the majority of our operations with the revenue we make.)

In order to start your own business you first have to be honest with yourself about whether you're cut out for it. If you just want to be your own boss for the headlines, the attention, and to be able to click "entrepreneur" in the career field when you fill out an online questionnaire, don't even try. If you just want the money, the lifestyle could work for you, but no guarantees, because building a long-term brand is about so much more than dollars in and dollars out. Not to sound like a motivational quote, but you really do need the passion for your chosen project. However, if you want to start your own business because you feel like you have a good idea, the drive, and you just *know* deep down that you have it in you to ~~suffer~~ build a business, then it might be worth the work for you.

So devote some time to really feeling out why you want to start this business, and be honest with yourself, because trust us when we say that the motivation peaks on the day you announce your new venture with a celebratory Instagram post.

Businesses are defined by the people behind them. An entrepreneur's life is for the person who has passion, drive, and commitment. Giving a shit is like being a shark. If a shark stops moving, it dies. Likewise, if you stop giving a shit about your business, guess what? It also dies. If you're someone who sort of floats through life not caring about anything except when the next happy hour is, then the entrepreneur life is not for you. Which is totally fine, by the way . . . happy hour is like, really great. But if you choose to be an entrepreneur, you're probs going to miss a lot of them.

WHAT IT TAKES

So what does it take to start your own business? Lucky for you, we made a checklist.

You should think about doing your own thing if you:

_____ enjoy checklists like these.

_____ don't want to work for someone else.

_____ are okay with failing.

_____ can't imagine working for someone else ever or anymore.

_____ are committed to putting 100 percent effort into whatever the fuck you want to do.

_____ have a "good" idea.

_____ have a lot of personal stamina and mental toughness (ask your friends if they think you have this).

_____ are confused why no one else is doing it.

_____ are cool with being bombarded by emails all fucking day.

_____ are prepared to not get a spa pedicure for the next three years.

Notice how we left out being well connected and graduating from business school, but not in a bad way. Truthfully, business school is a glorified social club for future entrepreneurs. It's a place where you can meet your potential business partner or connect yourself to someone who will hire you in the future. It's also a great way to have your parents spend $100,000 so you can take two years and travel to places like Japan, where you get wasted while "learning" about different business methods in foreign cultures. But nothing you'll learn in business school is comparable to the experiences you have actually working at your own company. No offense, but it's true.

A NOTE ON BUSINESS SCHOOL

We didn't go to business school, and while our opinion on it might seem a bit harsh for a place we haven't been, we have never heard an alternative opinion from actual business school graduates. Like literally not one. Not even the Harvard ones. Consider it research.

ACTUALLY STARTING YOUR BUSINESS

Now that you've fully evaluated yourself and decided that starting your own company is the right move, the rest is only harder, so get excited—yayyyy!

Come up with an idea: Since we can't sit here and help brainstorm an idea for you (we charge like, a billion an hour per founder for that type of shit), what we can do is help you figure out if you have stumbled onto a good idea.

The idea is a good one if . . . It is a completely brand-new idea and no one else is doing it. It has to feel so weird to you that no one's developed it yet that you have to google it to see if it exists, but it doesn't and you're like, *Fuck, am I like, a genius? Or am I just really stoned?* This is when people usually talk about "white spaces," but we like to call them blank spaces because we aren't racist and also that's like the best music video ever.

or

It's an upgraded version of something that already exists. Upgrade can mean a lot of things. You could be fixing something that you don't think is done correctly and that you feel you can do better. You could be making something more efficient, operationally and/or financially. You could just be improving the quality of something or taking a preexisting business model and applying it to a product that you think needs it, blah, blah, blah. If you were able to pay attention to what we just said, well then, that's a good sign you're ready for the business world. But if two sentences into this paragraph you just went straight to rewatching your own Insta story, you should stay in your PR job.

In all scenarios, you need to be solving a problem. No, it doesn't need to be something as momentous as world poverty. It could be something as simple as: "Oh, there are no makeup bloggers who take inspo from famous clowns! I know people would love that and I'm definitely the person to start it because I grew up doing makeup in a circus." Yes, that sounds stupid, but we promise, dumber business ideas exist. Everything is stupid until it's not. Imagine being in the room when the creator of almond milk was like, *I know people love milk, I know there's a world-famous ad campaign with super-famous people who "got milk," but what if from now on milk was made out of . . . get this . . . almonds!* Don't let the fear of no one being interested stop you from doing your thing.

After you are set on an idea, you need to research your "market." What this means is that you'll have to google a lot of things. Or bing it, we don't know your life.

The goal of market research is to find out if there's a demand for your idea, how large that potential demand is, and who your potential competitors are. In other words, this is the fucking boring part. If you have an adviser or mentor or someone who's done whatever you're about to do, the first thing you should do is get as much information as possible. Make sure to prepare a list of specific questions rather than vague open-ended ones such as, "So, like, what is market research?" If you don't have any help, use that list of questions you need answered and start looking things up online. Maybe pay for research or surveys. It's really important to be thorough, but like we said, it's sooooo boring. Again, if you can't get through this part, it's probably not going to work out for you, because you'll be doing things *way* more boring than this down the line.

MAKING IT REAL

Okay, so you have your idea, and it's all in your head, and you googled a bunch of stuff, and you're ready to make it offish. Stop it. Stop it right now. Don't touch the transfer-funds button yet. What you need to do is to define your business. Sometimes people call this coming up with an elevator pitch, but we avoid that term because there's nothing worse than people talking to us in an elevator, like, look at the floor light, move to the right, and shut the fuck up.

The definition of your business should be able to be explained in one to two concise sentences using everyday, non-business terms. With everyone's attention span decreasing by the minute, it's hard to captivate anyone's attention for any period of time, so keep it brief. Like someone really smart once said, if you can't explain it in thirty seconds or less, that means you don't understand it yourself. Also, it's a really useful practice to come up with what exactly you do or what your service provides at a very top level because it will focus your plan going forward. The worst thing that you can do when someone asks what is [insert your company name] is to start with a long-winded story about this idea you had when you were five and your Barbie had a bunch of clown-looking makeup and you really loved it. Yes, we're still using clown-makeup-blog analogy. No, we won't stop. Leave those anecdotal stories for when you're rich as fuck and you're being interviewed by Oprah.

If you come up with a quick way to define your company ASAP, then it'll be really easy to shut people up when they inevitably ask you why you quit your job, wondering if you're having a mental breakdown à la 2007 Britney.

Here's our short definition, for example: Betches Media is a digital media brand that creates extremely relatable, honest, and humorous content for millennial women across all digital and social platforms.

Chiseling your definition down to just one sentence is hard because it minimizes exactly what you do. We had so much trouble trying to define our business at first, mostly because the focus kept changing. People used to ask us what Betches was all the time, and we'd be like, "Ummm, we're like a website, a book, and a popular Instagram account . . . we write really funny stuff. You should check out our *Bachelor* recap! No, sorry, we forgot our business cards at home."*

But back to your idea. Once you define it concisely, it's time to ask people what they think about it. As opposed to market research, this part is super emotional. You have to take something you've been working on and see if people actually like it. Like, you have to be vulnerable and ask people for their

---

* We still always forget our business cards.

opinions and when they say, "I don't get it," you can't just be like, "Well, no one fucking asked you," because you did literally ask them.

This should be one of the only instances in life when you should really care about what other people think. Ask them questions, but more important, listen to their feedback. Don't be defensive. Save your attitude for conversations with your mom. Take notes, ask specific questions, but also listen to their generalized responses. Pass your idea on to people who you think would want to buy or use your product. Then ask other people who might have experience in investment, funding, or banking. Look for patterns in the feedback you get, like, if you keep getting "Eh, I wouldn't really use that" or "I feel like no one really has that issue" over and over again, well then, take the fucking hint. But if they say, "Who's your target consumer?" then answer them. If you haven't thought about it, then that person just helped you out because that's something you should be able to identify from the get-go.

After you've finalized your initial concept, go make that shit official. Like officially offish. Incorporation, bank account, a credit card that you're not going to be able to use as much as you want. This part is the easiest, as it's basically clerical work. If you're starting small, consider a limited liability company (LLC). Why? Find a friend who has an uncle who's a lawyer. He'll explain to you that almost all business decisions are made "for tax reasons." Go to the bank, open an account. Find a friend who has an uncle who's an accountant. Have him set you up so you can pay said taxes. The only part of all this that's not something Season One Peggy Olson couldn't do is come up with a name for your company. We can't do everything for you.

Inspirational Career Betch: Issa Rae

At the time I came up with the concept for ABG [Awkward Black Girl], I was just a clumsy, frustrated, socially inept, recently graduated adult, looking for confirmation that I wasn't alone. . . . As each new model for social media strives to connect us in new, paradoxically estranged ways, there exists a consistent core, the human desire to feel included. Whether you're an awkward black girl or an irritated disabled stripper, everyone should have the opportunity to feel represented in some way."
—Issa Rae, *The Misadventures of Awkward Black Girl*

Issa Rae is a writer, director, actress, and web series producer. Issa started out by raising money on Kickstarter and producing her own YouTube series, *The Misadventures of Awkward Black Girl*, which chronicles the firsthand stories of people of color. She created a show on HBO called *Insecure*, based on the awkward experiences of a modern African American woman, which we're personally huge fans of. Issa is a great example of someone who looked at the marketplace, didn't see people like herself represented, and decided to change that.

In her show, she talks about issues and topics that no one else is talking about from a perspective that many Americans don't get to see every day. She was able to capture the nuances of being a black woman in America and the African American struggle to succeed and overcome both blatant and subtle racism in a way that no one else could. Issa saw the standard depiction of African Americans and didn't see someone she thought represented her well and was tired of having to live up to "blackness" standards, when, as she says, "the very definition of 'blackness' is as broad as that of 'whiteness,' yet the media seemingly always tries to find a specific, limited definition."

Issa proves that if you think there are people like you with a different viewpoint not being represented, you can and should go out and depict them yourself. So if you don't see yourself represented in the world or you have a great idea to depict something that is lacking from the mainstream, write it, sing it, film it, paint it, or do whatever you need to do to share it with the world.

WORKING WITH FRIENDS

During this whole process, you'll probably have considered whether you can start something all on your own or if you'll need a Dionne to your Cher. News flash, the most important thing in business is knowing where you fall short and being very honest with yourself about those qualities. Because what you lack is exactly what you should look for in a partner(s). Let's just say you suck at financial stuff and the last thing you understand is "revenue diversification." That means you need a partner who thinks that shit is the most fun thing ever. They need to eat, sleep, and breathe finance and be more on top of it than when your mom reviews your credit card bill. The goal is to find nerds who complement your inner nerd.

Obviously it's really hard to know who to trust. The answer is no one. Like, most people have the capacity to fuck you over, no matter what industry you're in. Not to sound like Tony Soprano or Kristen Wiig in *Bridesmaids* but whatever. Really, lawyers are the only ones you can trust, and that's only because you pay them. No offense, but it's true. Remember Eduardo Saverin in *The Social Network*? He totally trusted Mark Zuckerberg, and look where that got him—in a courthouse fighting over a chicken cannibalism story that his supposed BFF planted about him. Also, Eduardo thought he was trusting his own lawyers in that story, but they were actually Facebook's lawyers and they ended up screwing him, too. See, trust no one.

Despite this, many people who are starting companies look to their friends or people they already know really well for help. This obviously has its pros and cons. We were best friends when we started Betches, and we haven't murdered each other yet, so it's definitely totally doable. But remember, a lot of work goes into a business relationship, just like any other relationship. One of the pros is that you're probably already honest with each other because you're friends and know each other's strengths and weaknesses without having to hear their bullshit answer about being "too much of a perfectionist." So instead of telling your friend she has some avocado on her face from lunch, you can channel that honesty by saying that you think she needs to be a stricter manager or whatever. The con is that your relationship will never be the same, obviously. Dun dun dun.

If you're both or all pulling equal weight then everything is amazing. But seriously imagine what will happen when one senses the other is slacking off. Things can turn into a shitstorm faster than that time you both showed up in the same dress to formal. The minute you guys do not agree on something is the minute when your relationship will be tested because you'll need to talk through your opinions professionally. As a general rule, keep your fights about work stuff and friendship stuff separate.

WAIT TILL YOU SEE MY DECK

A business deck is basically your business plan laid out in slides. We suggest PDF format because everyone hates accidentally opening PowerPoint. There's nothing worse than seeing that bouncing icon on your dock, followed by the dreaded

Microsoft Auto Update. Seriously, gag me with a spoon. Stick to PDF.

Your business plan should be brief, concise, and minimalistic, like a Scandinavian bedroom designed for Instagram. The last thing you want is to give someone a headache because of all your fucking clip art. PSA: Don't use clip art. Your deck should answer the following:

- What is your company?
- What problem does your company solve?
- How will it solve that problem?
- The market—who's your audience/customer and how big can that demographic get?
- Who's your competition and why are you better than them?
- Brag about your team, but only if they have bragging rights, a.k.a. they have legit and relevant experience. No, being their sorority recruitment chair doesn't count.
- Money: explain your business model and come up with projections for how much you plan to make in the next year and/or five years (if your goal isn't to make money right away, briefly describe why and how much money you will hypothetically make when you finally monetize).

- Use of funds: Create an ask, i.e., how much money do you want (if you're raising money) and then describe how you plan to use it over a defined period of time.

That was like a really dumbed-down guide, because every company is different and you should tailor each deck for the investor or partner who's going to be reading it. Also, to give a full rundown of how to make the perfect business plan would be a whole book in itself, but this should definitely get you started. And like everything else in the world, that shit can be found on Google. Put more simply: think about what would make someone want to give you money to build and grow your company and highlight those attributes when you present it.

IT'S LIKE *SHARK TANK*

Okay, so, this part is literally the worst if this isn't your thing, and we admit it's not ours, either. We're creative, funny people, not master fund-raisers. We're really good at making money but not great at asking people for it. But like we said, admitting that you suck at something makes it easier to focus on what you need to find. Pretending you're good at everything makes people think you're untrust-worthy and not self-aware. It's okay to admit that this is not your strength, while emphasizing the things that *are* your strengths. Humble brag.

There are so many different ways you can fund-raise: friends and family (think your parents and their/your friends who want to seem cool by being associated with your company), angel investors (think rich people who want to give you smaller amounts early in the game), venture capital (think big amounts that also require big returns), accelerator or incubator programs (think nudist colony but with clothes, money, and resources), and bank loans (think no equity in your business but interest rates).

Ultimately, you have to make the decision for yourself. Think about what type of network you have and who is in it. Rack your brain for people you know and who they might know. Don't be afraid to reach out to people for advice. If you know someone who is really rich who would be a great investor, or know someone who might know someone, request a meeting, but you should rarely ask for it with the purpose of getting investment. Instead, ask for advice. This person will be flattered and more likely give you five minutes of their time. During those five minutes show him or her the opportunity of your company by way of actually asking him or her a legitimate question that he or she has the capacity to answer. It's not that asking for money directly is bad; in fact, in some cases it's important to get straight to the point. If you're making a meeting with a bunch of venture capitalists, of course everyone knows why you're there, so prepare a pitch presentation. But if you're meeting with someone you know, don't treat it like an official pitch meeting. That can turn that person off and you will get neither advice nor money. Come to that type of meeting with your pitch and top-line financials memorized so you'll be able to answer questions on the spot.

Remember, when you receive money via investment, you'll most likely have to give away some ownership of your company. That's called equity, duh, and it's just the cost of doing business. Let's say you decide to make weed-infused chocolate chip cookies. Your friend sees you baking and is like, "I have a weed infuser that will make twelve times as many weed cookies with less effort." You're like, "Yeah, that sounds great, thanks so much!" But now you have to give your friend half of your weed cookies. In this specific metaphor that made us both hungry and in the mood to smoke, accepting your friend's use of their weed infuser is equivalent to gaining an investor in your company. You got their money, but they get to take ownership of some of your business. It's up to you to decide how much say you want to give to anyone else and what you're willing to sacrifice for their money.

> *Ask for money, get advice. Ask for advice, get money twice.*
> —Pitbull, "Feel This Moment"

A NOTE ON INVESTOR MEETINGS

Once you start taking meetings with potential investors, expect them to ask you what your final goal is, or what your exit strategy is. What they mean is *Who are potential buyers of your company? Who's going to want what you have? And why?* Have an answer for them. PS: "I came, I saw, I left early" is *not* an exit strategy.

THE REST

Think of starting your own business like getting married. Writing your business plan and figuring out your moneymaking strategy is sort of like your engagement. What people don't talk about is that after the wedding you have to like, be married for a really long time. After you're done with your deck, you now actually have to build this company and grow it, appease these investors, deal with potentially crazy employees, etc.

Like we said, that takes a certain type of person. If that's not you, just be real with yourself and don't do it. But if the only thing holding you back is fear of failing, get the fuck over it. Failing is no big deal. Steve Jobs failed a lot, which a lot of people seem to forget takes up a significant portion of his long-ass biography. The most successful people fail all the time; it just means they're willing to take risks that the people stuck in their monotonous nine-to-fives are too afraid to take.

THE MOTHERFUCKING HUSTLE

Can everyone please stop talking about how much they love the hustle? Unless you're in an interview, in all likelihood, no one fucking cares. Most people who actually "hustle" don't waste their time bragging about it. They're actually out there working hard. Literally anytime someone says "I just love the hustle" to us, we're all just thinking, *Cool, do you want a cookie?*

To hustle means to focus on a goal and do literally everything possible you can to achieve it. Not taking rejection or no for an answer, not stopping until you reach that goal, even to post an inspirational instagram that your friends are secretly screenshotting and mocking you for. Hustling is persistence, dedication, and stepping out of your comfort zone. It's a real mindset, one that is a key factor for success that people have been practicing forever.

Hustling is not easy, nor is it Insta-friendly. So the reason why this word has such a bad aftertaste is because it's been diluted and ruined by people on social media who just talk about hustling without actually living it. If you're posting about hustling, you're not actually doing work, you're procrastinating. Fucking duh.

SPEAKING OF SIDE HUSTLES . . .

From the PR girl who dreams of being a makeup influencer to the finance betch who wants to start her own fund, the only thing standing in the way of making a side hustle into your reality is you. Yikes, did we just type that?

Whether the obstacle is getting started, or you're going full steam but can't pull the trigger to make this your main priority, there will always be something standing in your way.

So here are two ideas that you should remember if you want to turn your side gig into your full-time gig:

1. **It can't just be a hobby.** Sure, you have to love what you're doing, but even more important than that is your belief that it will be successful. Being emotionally fulfilled does not offer financial security unless you live in a tent and meditate all day. Beyond passion, you need to have confidence in the skills that pertain to making your project a successful business. Remember, being passionate about something doesn't mean that you're good at it. Exhibit A: every bro you know is obsessed with football; almost none are professional athletes. Almost always when you turn something you love into your 24/7 job, it becomes exactly that: a job. Taking pictures of your fancy clothes with OOTD captions is a lot less fun when your rent money depends on it.

2. **You need to commit.** You can't be half in. You can't make excuses because it's going to be stressful. When working on a startup, the workweek isn't forty hours, it's one hun-

dred hours, minimum. Use that as your guide. Work on the weekends, work at night, say no to brunch, it'll be devastating, you'll be fine.

But once you realize that you have something worth quitting your day job for, commit yourself and quit. You'll know when it's time to quit when your side hustle starts to seep into your day job. It'll feel like it requires a lot more attention than you're able to give while working a full-time job. That's when we suggest you take the plunge, especially if you're young and don't have like, a mortgage or eight kids (ugh).

TL;DR

A lot of people dream of starting their own businesses. A lot even go as far as discussing how they'd hypothetically make that business work with their friends. But rarely do they dive in headfirst because it's honestly really scary. Believing in yourself, your ideas, and your ability to succeed is one of the most important obstacles to overcome when starting. You have to have the courage to be like, *Fuck yeah, this could be good. I could be good.* Once you get that part out of the way, the rest is busy work.

Dear Betches,

I have a slight obsession with skin care. I love everything about lotions, oils, serums—not only the products, but I actually enjoy researching the ingredients, etc. I have helped several friends with their skin-care issues and many of them have encouraged me to start a blog. I have almost flawless skin, because of my years of cultivating a specific yet evolving skin-care regimen—so I do know my shit. I think that this would be a great way for me to have a creative outlet with something that I am passionate about in my free time.

So my questions is, how did you all know when you had something that was worth starting and sharing with the world? How did you decide to take the leap and what was the progress like? How did this whole thing unfold for the Betches blog/website/podcast? Obvi a skin-care blog wouldn't necessarily be as universal as your business, but I am interested in the trajectory of the Betches to see if that could help give me the confidence and also maybe what to expect in starting this.

Thank you!!

Sincerely,
Flawless-Face Betch

Dear Flawless-Face Betch,

The road to starting a new business definitely isn't easy, but if you have enough passion and are willing to work hard, you're much more likely to see success. We started Betches when we were in college and therefore had no income to lose anyway. We were lucky in that we didn't have families to support or rent to pay, so we were able to focus exclusively on building our brand and putting out great content that was consistent and that our audience loved. Early on, we found a book agent who believed we had something special and helped us create a proposal to shop to various publishers.

It wasn't always so glamorous, though. After graduating, we moved home and would write from our parents' houses because we weren't making enough money to move out and into our own apartments. At times, it seemed really tough to watch others move ahead while we were working on something we weren't positive would succeed.

However, we knew there was an audience for the things we were talking about and that gave us the faith to write a book proposal and eventually sell our first book to Simon & Schuster. We were getting really positive feedback from the Betches community, which encouraged us to not give up and to hang in there until our business was profitable.

For you, it seems like skin care is something you're really

passionate about. If you feel like you're doing something or could do something in the world of skin care that hasn't been done before and that there's a market for and can sustain yourself financially, you should definitely pursue it as a business. Make it your side hustle and spend all your free time cultivating your skin-care line or blog. You have to be willing to sacrifice some free time and potentially some money in order to see if this could really work out for you.

Then, if you feel like the world is responding well and people are gaining something from what you have to do or say, keep at it. Don't worry about how you're going to make a million dollars and have a million readers at first, just worry about how you can potentially grow your income to start out and how to deliver for the audience you have. That's the only way to get it off the ground at first, and then see where it goes. The best ideas come when you're truly focused on your project and how to make it better, not on what everyone else is doing and how they're currently more successful than you. Don't give up when it feels like you're plateauing, and channel that passionate energy into doing what you love and hopefully you can eventually make a career out of it. Be realistic with yourself. It's not nearly as exciting as what you see on TV or social media, but if you believe in your product and you're willing to give it all you've got, then it's definitely worth a shot.

Good luck!
Betches

7.
LET'S TAKE THIS OFFLINE

Working in the Digital Age

Before the internet, the only tools employers had for figuring out if you were a complete freak before they hired you were your résumé, cover letter, and interview style. Needless to say, shit has changed a lot since the dawn of the twenty-first century. When employers are considering you for a job, there's a negative 100,000 percent chance that they won't stalk your social media accounts. Based on your online presence, your potential boss can and will gauge what type of person you are in your personal life, because aside from articles written about you that they find through a Google search, everything else is a self-curated digital portrayal of your personality. Your Instagram, anything you retweet, and any pictures of you taken at events are all signals of the type of person you are trying to be perceived as. You better believe they will judge the shit out of the ten thirst-trap bikini pics you posted to make your ex jealous.

First, they'll look at your LinkedIn because it's the most professional version of you. So, if your LinkedIn profile is a selfie with your boobs popping out of your tank top, they won't look any further. Save that shit for your dating profile. Your LinkedIn profile picture doesn't necessarily have to be a professional headshot, but it should be a cutout of your face—from above the boobs to the top of the head. Don't include your friends, family, or significant other, and make sure your head isn't tilted like ninety degrees because you think that's how you look good when in reality you actually look like Meryl Streep in *Death Becomes Her*.

Next, they'll quickly do a Google search to make sure no concerning headlines about you come up like *Sophomore Girl Arrested for Performing Oral Sex in College Bar Bathroom*. If that's the case and you're trying to get a job, there are Google-search Olivia Popes available to you in this world who can help move that search down. As employers, we think it's definitely worth it to pay for them if you have the resources.

Next, they'll go to Facebook. These days, Facebook accounts don't tell you much. Most people keep things private anyway, so this will most likely just be a quick glance at your profile picture. Pictures with your significant other or friends are fine here, since Facebook profiles are intended to be more personal. As long as your (hopefully nonexistent) politically driven posts are private, them dropping by your page won't really affect you. And, duh, don't blindly accept friend requests, the requestor could be someone from the company. If that happens, set your profile to be super private, and then accept. But honestly it would be weird if they did that, so it's probably just a Russian hooker and you shouldn't accept anyway. Facebook friends are so 2013.

Also, you're not being fucking stealth by changing your last name to your middle name on Facebook, Don Draper. You changing your name to Melissa Ashley on Facebook hides nothing, and an employer can still easily find your Facebook profile with a simple Google search, so make sure your public visibility is limited.

Next: Instagram. This platform poses a lot of potential problems because tons of people aren't private in the hopes that someone will discover them and they'll become the next Gigi Hadid. Unless your mother is Yolanda Hadid or Kim Kardashian, cut this shit out. While we don't want to tell you not to ~~live~~ insta your life, you need to have boundaries if you're employed or hoping to be employed. Even if you think you have the coolest boss ever, the number of selfies you put up will not go unnoticed. In fact, we're already definitely judging you. But if you're trying to get employed, it's super important that your profile isn't just selfies or pictures with your ass out, because that's the number one sign you're a huge narcissist or like, don't have any friends. Both aren't great.

Companies want to see that you're either a private person or that the contents of what you share are harmless, especially if your job is client facing. Like if your bio reads, *Fuck bitches, get money,* HR of your *not*-future company will be highly concerned. An employer just wants to see that you're "normal," which obviously is a really general term. They want to see that you're a socially competent person and not a liability.

How to achieve that:

DO: Post pics with friends.
DON'T: Post only selfies.

DO: Post an Instagram story of you putting on a face mask.
DON'T: Post an Instagram story of you face-planting when blackout drunk.

DO: Post a pic in a bikini on a pool float.
DON'T: Post a pic of you in a bikini getting a champagne shower from a tan old dude in a pool.

DO: Post a quote you like.

DON'T: Post hateful shit from extremist groups.

DO: Post pics of your food.

DON'T: Post pics of your boobs.

And finally, they'll do a quick look at Twitter to make sure you don't tweet anything like, creepy.

EMAIL ETIQUETTE

Email is the number one way people communicate in business right now. Back in the day it used to be phone calls and martini lunches. Now it's eat lunch at your desk while you get back to your five hundred emails, so it's really important that you're good at writing them. Some people are born with the skill of crafting beautifully written, strongly worded emails. We are definitely three of them. Then there are people who literally are the worst. And there are a lot of different ways you can be the absolute worst at emails. Let's go through them:

The No-Contexter

Self-explanatory, but this person will email you without any fucking context. It's honestly the most annoying thing a coworker, especially a boss, can receive. When crafting an email (or really, any type of message) it's important to think about how your message will be received, not just how you want to write it. If you send an email that literally sounds like you were midthought and you sent only the second half of it expecting them to just know what you're talking about, you're crazy. If you want to write in shorthand, that's fine, but at least tell the recipient what you're referring to. Put a fucking *RE:* in the subject line. If you do choose to send a half-assed email, the person you sent it to most likely won't understand and will email you back *Wait, sorry what?*, and then you'll have to explain it anyway and you'll be the one who'll look like the idiot.

The Bad Intro'er

Every day, people connect through email. If you're helping a friend or colleague by providing them with something they want via an intro, then great, you're doing something right. But if a friend or acquaintance asks you to intro them to someone who'd normally be very out of reach, hesitate. The person receiving that random email then has to like, take time out of their day to respond to something that they most likely don't have time for as a favor to someone they literally don't know. Be careful with the intros you make. Wasting intros corrodes your relationship with the person who is receiving the unwanted email and potentially puts you in a weaker position with them in the future, which can hurt your own career. You wouldn't just set up your friend with an ugly, boring guy without running it by her first, right? Right. Both ends of the intro should at least somewhat benefit from being introduced, and if you don't think they will, just be like *Sorry, can't help you.*

If you feel really bad saying no but you also don't feel comfortable making the intro, you have to figure out which will hurt you more, making the intro (thus hurting your relationship with this very busy, important person), or declining to make the intro (likely to a friend or someone else asking for a favor who you don't want to disappoint). If you're having trouble navigating the situation, take the course of action that will hurt you less long-term. Of course, you always want to be supportive, but requests to be intro'ed should be appropriate. If you're comfortable with it, you have the option of warning the person you're sending the intro to ahead of time to let them know it's coming and feel free to make sure they're okay with it.

The Oversharer

Listen, we get it. When you want something from someone and you get connected to them, it's really easy to want to just be like, *Thanks for connecting, here are my problems, please fix them.* But unfortunately, that person is going to be like, *Who the fuck are you? Why would I help you?* and ignore your email. (Unless, of course, that person sees an opportunity for themselves in exchange for this favor. Yes, everyone is selfish, get used to it.) No one wants to help anyone out of the goodness of their hearts. Everyone has shit to do and is busy. As Phoebe Buffay proved, there's no such thing as a selfless good deed.

So if a mutual friend connects you to someone who can help you, simply say, "Thanks for the connection," give a brief overview of what you want to discuss with this person veiled with a form of flattery, then ask when they're available to get on a fifteen-minute call. Example: *Thanks, XYZ, for connecting us! Moving you to BCC. Hi, ABC, so nice to be connected. I've always admired your work in [insert whatever the fuck they do]. I'm developing my own [insert whatever the fuck you are doing] and would love to get your feedback. Let me know when you're free for a quick fifteen-minute chat. Looking forward! [Your name]*

See what we did there? You made them feel not only cool but also like their opinion is important. You also didn't waste their time with paragraphs of boring shit about what you do and what you're looking for, and you didn't ask for an insane amount of help at the first introduction via email. To reiterate, they don't know you yet, so they don't give a fuck. Once you're on the phone, you can literally say whatever because you've hooked them for fifteen minutes; ask for your favor then.

CALENDAR INVITE ETIQUETTE

When inviting anyone to anything, keep in mind that this person now has to have that invitation sitting on their calendar. So when they go look at their calendar, and they see their own name, and the word *meeting* next to it, they're like *WTF is this? Delete.* Again, context. When you're initiating a meeting, write both of your names as the title, a dash or your punctuation of choice, and a few words detailing your meeting like *Q2 Budget Chat.* And if you're putting something on your boss's or coworker's calendar, make sure to write a description of this meeting's existence in the notes and don't do it without looking to see if they're busy or asking them directly first. If your calendar etiquette continues to miss the mark, your boss might start to wonder if you're this careless when you communicate externally on behalf of the company. Then all of a sudden you're fired and you wish you could go back to the days when all you had to do was correctly update the location of a client lunch and learn.

WORK PHRASES AND WHAT
THEY REALLY MEAN

The thing about professional environments is that you can never say what you really mean, otherwise everyone will think you're an asshole, a psycho, or both. In an effort to create a work life that doesn't resemble the scene in *Mean Girls* where the Plastics' burn book gets distributed to the whole school, the following fake AF phrases were born.

Sorry for the delayed response = I read your email quickly last week and completely forgot about it. And I didn't give a fuck.

Circle back = Let's revisit this when both parties care enough to think about it. Please just stop talking to me about it now.

Any update here? = CAN YOU ANSWER ME, ASSHOLE?

Let's do a deep dive = Let's not.

This past week has been hectic over here! = Literally nothing has happened, I just forgot about your email.

Mind sending a calendar invite? = I'm too lazy to do it myself. I don't want to be on this call as badly as you apparently do, so you should do all the work.

Hope all is well! = Please just don't tell me if it's not.

HOW TO SLACK LIKE A WORK BETCH

If you don't already know what Slack is, you're probably in the medical or financial field, use Instagram as a job, or are like, a starving artist. Slack is a major intercompany communication tool that's basically one big group chat. Side note: RIP, Gchat, we barely knew thee. A lot of shit can happen in Slack. We personally love the platform because we love watching employees troll each other in our #random thread.

While work-trolling is really fun (depending on your company culture) make sure your boss doesn't see that you're constantly slacking about nonwork topics, because, don't forget: Slack isn't AIM. Your employers have access to all your Slack conversations. On top of that, if you're talking shit about someone in Slack (or on iMessage), and you're presenting something or just sharing your screen with someone in a meeting and then that notification shows up, you're super fucked. It's the work equivalent of sending your crush a screenshot of your own conversation—awkward.

Speaking of iMessage, if you have it connected to your computer, then do everyone a favor and turn off notifications. (If you don't know how to do that, then fucking look it up, this isn't an Apple tech-support pamphlet.) You're not hiding anything by having group chats excluding your annoying coworkers—everyone notices when five people whose notifications just went off at the same time start randomly laughing. Also, your boss doesn't have to be Harriet the fucking Spy to know you're talking shit about something they just told you to do when right after they finish speaking, you get a message on your screen with the group chat name FUCK THIS PLACE.

Also, stop online shopping or adding stuff to your registry on your computer; do it on your phone where no one will notice. People's posture in front of a computer changes when they're doing something for work versus when they're doing something for fun. If suddenly you go from hunched over and lifeless to leaning forward and scrolling furiously, we all know you're looking for flights to Cabo. Make sure that you're confident in your body language before you shop for a crop top during work hours.

INAPPROPRIATE THINGS TO SAY ON WORK CHANNELS

We get it, all you want to do all day is either talk shit about Linda in sales, go over lunch options, or discuss the guy you hooked up with last night. If you're not someone who gives a shit about things like ambition, working hard, or your career, that's fine, but you have to hide that at work, especially when chatting in Slack or email, where everything you do is company property.

Inappropriate Shit You Shouldn't Type at Work

- Talk about who you had sex with last night.
- Talk about having sex with someone from work last night in full detail.

- Complain about the work you have to do.
- Make fun of coworkers you think are weird.
- Gang up on a coworker because she smells bad or uses the wrong form of *they're*.
- Bitch about your boss, obviously.

A NOTE ON USING DATING APPS TO NETWORK

You should absolutely do this. We don't mean *only* use dating apps to network, but if the world gives you an opportunity to connect with strangers online, then why should you only use it to find someone to sleep with? Why not use it to advance your network and career? Let's say you start messaging with someone and they happen to tell you what they do, and you feel like this person might be someone worth meeting (obviously google them before deciding), you should consider a date. By no means are we saying have sex with someone in order to network. Just go on a date, figure out who they are, what they like, and make a friend. Then, if there's no romantic connection but you still really want to work with them, sign them on as a client, or just have them in your network, it's okay to wait a week, then text asking for their email address. Be like *I know this is random, but I know you had mentioned [quote something they had mentioned about their job during your date] and I think there's an interesting way we could work together.* Then send the eggplant emoji. JK.

While that tactic kind of sounds manipulative because

you knew you weren't that interested from the start, people do way worse shit on dating apps. Just think of all the guys who know they're not interested in a relationship and just want to have sex but say otherwise to get girls in bed. Same shit. Plus, our idea is way more benign. You're only being deceptive in that you want to put a meeting on the calendar next Tuesday, how's 2:00–3:00 p.m.?

HR NIGHTMARE: THE INFLUENCER

If you don't ever want to care about the appropriateness of your Slack messages, calendar invites, or emails with coworkers, become an influencer.* Not to get all Carrie Bradshaw, but with so many people on Instagram telling you to click the link in their bio to get a discount on sunglasses, we couldn't help but wonder: What does it even mean to be an influencer anymore?

Generally, in order to be considered an influencer, a person has to be influential, as in their opinion convinces someone else to think a certain way or buy a certain thing. And we don't mean your grandma who you convinced to get a MacBook, but more like your peers who want to buy the cute

---

* Keyword here is *coworkers*. Since influencers work from their phones, they have to master email communication.

shoes you're wearing and shit. It's kind of weird that being an influencer is so accessible that anyone with an iPhone and a photo-editing app can become "famous" now. The dream of peddling bear-shaped candy that makes your hair grow on the internet can be anyone's! Ah, America.

If you're just another girl posting pics of her ass in tiny shorts with captions like *Being extra cheeky today,* we don't recommend you quit your day job—if you even still have one at this point. We're all for expressing yourself and your sexuality, but it doesn't make sense to act one way on Instagram and another in your real life. Like, if you work in finance by day and as an amateur ass model on Instagram at night, the clear disconnect in your life won't get you anywhere. But if you work in fashion and like to post high-end lingerie from relevant brands on your page, then maybe you could use your day job to your advantage later on if you ever decide to turn your side hustle account into a real hustle.

So how do you know if the influencer life is for you? If you actually have a unique skill or perspective, then go for it. Start your Instagram on the side. If you're very consistent in your posts and aesthetic and actually see that people like your content, it's very possible to "make it" on Instagram. And by make it we mean graduate from peddling vitamins to peddling luxury cars and potentially getting recognized at Coachella.

TL;DR

Now that everything has moved completely online, understanding how to navigate digital communication professionally should be a priority if it isn't already. Don't communicate with your boss via DM, don't send pointless emails without context, don't send calendar invites with half the pertinent info missing, just don't do it. Also please don't text about anything work related because it's very hard to keep track of. Texts disappear all the time, it's like making plans on Snapchat. Inevitably you'll start talking about something else and forget to write down the work-related thing you just planned, and—poof!—there goes your performance bonus. And if you hate all of this and prefer to be an HR nightmare, become an influencer.

Inspirational Betchy Historical Event: The Sony Hack

On November 24, 2014, a hacker group released confidential scripts, personal information, and internal emails from Sony Pictures. Included in this leak was everything from employees' Social Security numbers to fights with North Korean leader Kim Jong Un about the movie *The Interview*, to fucked-up emails from Sony executives about actors and scripts. In one email, producer Scott Rudin referred to Angelina Jolie as a "minimally talented spoiled brat" because she wanted David Fincher to direct *Cleopatra* instead of the Steve Jobs movie Rudin preferred him to direct. Wow, way harsh, Tai. There's also another fucked-up, pretty racist back-and-forth about which movies starring predominantly African American actors Amy Pascal should be sure to mention before her meeting with Barack Obama at a referenced "stupid" fund-raising event. Pascal had to resign quickly after the leak, and Sony was hit with a shit ton of lawsuits from its employees because so much of their personal info was disseminated.

The lesson here is that it's not just immature betches who talk a ton of shit. Everyone does it, so just be smart about it. Don't put anything in a work email that you wouldn't want released to the public. A hacked and released company email is like a three-way-calling attack on crack. Only instead of Karen finding out that you think she needs attention, Angelina Jolie might find out that you insinuated that she's a spoiled little bitch and never wants to work with your sexist ass again. Emails can get you into a shit ton of trouble even if you're innocent and no one will ever read them. Just ask Hillary Clinton.

Dear Betches,

I am emailing you because I recently (about six months ago) started a new job on a team of eleven. I was placed in a two-person department where the other person is super needy and clingy AF—help! He was really shy and quiet when he was training me but has now gotten comfortable . . . too comfortable. He is in his early twenties, and this is his first "real" job since graduating university. He follows me everywhere, so much so that when I'm by myself people in other divisions ask where my sidekick is. I don't think he has a crush or anything because he referred to himself as my "not-gay gay best friend." Weird. Plus, he knows I am engaged. It's becoming too much for me, but my subtle hints are not working.

Details: He does some weird stuff like asks what days I bring a lunch and what days I go out so he can do the same. If I go with someone else for lunch, he will skip his and eat at his desk alone. He does have other friends in the office, so I don't understand. If I don't talk to him first thing in the morning, he will send me an email to ask if I am tired because I'm "being quiet." One time I said I was going to get my eyebrows done on break, and he asked to come with me. Umm, no. He sends me emails all day about nonwork stuff that I have started to ignore, but since I haven't been answering, he sends double the amount. At first, I was responding to them because I was trying to fit in, but I really just want to go to work and do my thing. I am aiming for a promotion and want to show my independence and make sure the managers know I don't rely on him or his help.

He even recently told the managers we needed to sit together to be more efficient, so they moved me to the cubicle beside his. I can't get away! I have asked the managers to switch me to a different department and said it was for a learning opportunity, but they think he and I are very efficient together. But he has started to dump all the work on me. He will lie about the amount of work he has to do, and when I call him out on it he just laughs it off. When he is off for a day, I cover him, but when I am off, he doesn't cover me. I'm getting really annoyed at having to do his work on top of my own, but it reflects badly on me if it's not done. I think the worst thing was he canceled his vacation time to stay at work and told the managers it was because the department was behind, and he didn't want me to struggle on my own. None of which is true—which I told the managers, but the damage was done.

So how do I approach this guy to tell him to back off? Any small comments I have said so far, he turns around to make me look bad or makes it a joke. Please help!

Sincerely,
Independence-Seeking Betch

Dear Independence,

No doubt your coworker sounds really annoying, but don't worry, we're here to help. This is a great example of how working in the digital age can actually help you achieve your goal here. The first thing you need to do is write your coworker a detailed email about his transgressions. Let him know his constant small talk is getting in the way of your productivity, and express your disappointment at learning that he has given your managers the false impression that you are not pulling your weight despite all the evidence proving otherwise. State as many examples of this "evidence" as you can remember and have proof

of, and include this information in the email. Hopefully, this will be a wake-up call for him and will push him to shape up and act more professionally.

If he doesn't respond in an appropriate manner and change his ways after this email, you now have a logged digital attempt on your part to smooth things over, and you can and should feel free to present this to your bosses. You should also show them the continuous emails and texts that he's sent you that distract you and display his clinginess. By holding on to these emails, you now have proof that he sucks, and it'll be up to your managers to take the appropriate action. If you just go to your bosses without any written-out information, it will be his word against yours, make you seem whiny, and leave you in the same position that you were in when he blamed you for being behind in your work.

We get that this is hard, as it's often awkward and uncomfortable to call someone out on their shitty behavior, and it can be easier to just deflect or ignore it. If the problem is big enough that it's affecting how your performance is being perceived, that means it's necessary to be direct.

Hopefully this will leave you enough time to get your eyebrows threaded in peace and continue to kill it at work without being someone's scapegoat.

Good luck!
Betches

8.
WARMEST REGARDS

Women and Men at Work

A long, long time ago, a bunch of cave bros got together and decided how things would work in cave society. Like any legit economist, these cave bros figured out that specialization is key. If their cave families had any chance of surviving the harsh prehistoric conditions, they would have to figure out how to feed, clothe, and shelter themselves efficiently in order to sustain their offspring and perpetuate their *amazing* male genes.

With the obvious anatomical differences and males' lack of capacity to birth children, it was clear whose job was whose. Men would be the ones to provide resources for the home/cave (which in those days meant food, not exotic island vacations and walk-in closets to house your various purses), while women would be the ones to use those resources to manage and sustain the home/cave. These jobs were pretty obvious, as men are physically stronger and therefore better equipped to hunt and fish relative to women; meanwhile, women were the only ones even remotely physically equipped to continue our species. Seems pretty fucking important. In fact, we have a slight intuition that it was the males' inability to even attempt the latter responsibility that got them worked up and needing to assert their dominance. The cave bros had to take action and defend their job territory in any way they could, on the off chance that women might start providing for the families better than they did, and then women would be in charge of both the baby-birthing *and* the hunting. And then what would men even be necessary for, outside of providing sperm? (Which, let's face it, are a dime a dozen.) Welcome to ground zero of male insecurity, a feeling that has probably been at the root of thousands of sexual harassment lawsuits.

So what started out as an anatomical difference that, when you really think about it, shows that women are actually *more* evolutionarily useful than men, has somehow become the foundation of vast workplace inequalities that persist to this day. This dynamic has existed throughout history as bros convinced themselves that if women were allowed to have jobs and drive cars, then men would never get hard again or some such bullshit, and thus the patriarchy was born. The patriarchy is all around us and is constantly trying to hold women down through things like unequal pay, sexual harassment, and disparities in child-care responsibilities. One can even argue that the societal emphasis placed on women's appearances hinders our career advancement by convincing us that we need to concentrate on looking insanely hot at all times, thereby wasting our time applying twenty different cosmetic products each day and endlessly counting calories, which wastes the time and mental headspace that we could be using to actually get shit done.

> Men are raised to worry about their legacies, not their upper arm and thigh fat, stretch marks, crows-feet, saggy elbows, ugly armpits, thin eyelashes, and normal-smelling genitals. This is how society keeps us out of the C-suite—it booby-traps the way to the top with self-loathing, then reroutes us on a never-ending path of self-improvement.
>
> —Jessica Knoll, *The Favorite Sister*

Luckily, as we discussed in the earlier chapter on the history of women at work, the workplace has slowly started to change. Modern feminism has led to people fighting on the daily for things like getting paid the same amount as bros for the equivalent work they do, and to go to work without their boss groping them in exchange for letting them keep their job. TBH, we don't know how it's taken so long to get where we are, but like any douchebag you know would say, *it is what it is*, and that's just the reality we have to work with. Given that we've only been on a similar level to men in terms of employment rates for about forty years, men have had a shit ton of time to learn how to do things like network and ask for raises, while women are playing catch-up and navigating a workforce that their mothers and grandmothers were barely invited to. I mean, until 1978 women could be *legally* fired from their jobs just for getting pregnant. And you thought morning sickness was bad.

We also have to deal with men who can't handle the fact that we're just as good if not better than them at many jobs, and who still hold outdated opinions that women shouldn't be in power. Sorry, assholes, but we're no longer chilling in the cave all day making you sandwiches. We're working overtime at the office (ugh) and ordering Sweetgreen salads that we can now pay for ourselves.

While we've made some progress, we're still up against many of the same forces that have always worked against us. For the majority of history, women were primarily judged on how they looked and their ability to have and take care of their kids. Now, we are lucky enough to still be judged on those points and get the added benefit of being critiqued on our work performance, attitude, and ability to do it all with a smile on our faces. Women at work are expected to be devoted mothers and wives, have full-time jobs, and look amazing, all while appearing modest and never talking ourselves up too much or coming off as "too aggressive."

Being the perfect woman, though, is impossible to achieve and sets us up for failure and feeling terrible about ourselves. In fact, it's pretty fucking contradictory. How can we get ahead without advocating for ourselves? How can we remember to attach cover sheets to all our TPS reports if we're busy trying not to trip on our own heels, get our hair colored to cover those stress grays, and text while watching every one of our daughter's soccer games? How can we tell our coworkers that their ideas are shitty if we're going to be criticized for being too bossy and controlling? How can we support our families while being afraid that our success will emasculate the men around us? We can't and we shouldn't be expected to.

Michelle Wolf perfectly captures the catch-22 of being a modern working mother in her *Nice Lady* comedy special on HBO: "You're having a baby? Great. Couple things . . . We're going to need you to get that car accident of a body back to work as soon as possible, because this is America and we don't think you need time to recover. Also, you should breastfeed because that's what's best for the baby. But don't do it in public, you pig! Do it in the old janitor's closet with the rest of the breastfeeding trolls. And don't ask to take time off from work when your kids are sick. We'll think you're not dedicated. Also, why are you such a bad mom? By the way, your salary is just enough to cover the cost of childcare. And we know you're exhausted and you don't know who you are anymore trying to balance your old life and your new life, but, quick! Go have sex with your husband! He's about to leave! He doesn't understand what you're going through! Quick, go now! And, sweetie, smile!"

Obviously, not every industry is created equal when it comes to female treatment and representation. Fields like fashion, PR, and law have a leg up when it comes to examples of strong, powerful depictions of women (just ask Anna Wintour, who's been the HBIC at *Vogue* since before we were born). Fields like finance and engineering, on the other hand, have a long way to go. It's up for debate why some fields are more male-dominated than others. Some claim that women are biologically more drawn to certain fields than others, but these are also the jobs that are hardest to break into as a woman. So what came first, the chicken or the eggs you should freeze so you don't have to worry about having a baby while focusing on your career?

In addition to being harder to crack into, fields like finance contain a ton of boy's club–esque norms. In such a hypermasculine environment, men can be aggressive, mostly give a shit about money, and think it's chill to act like animals to impress each other. On the other hand, women seem to be drawn toward more nurturing-oriented jobs such as teaching, nursing, and social work. Is it true that women are inherently more concerned with being a decent human being and

> *I guess some people object to powerful depictions of awesome ladies.*
>
> —Leslie Knope,
> *Parks and Recreation*

giving back to the world than our male counterparts? I mean, probably, and I fucking hope so.

Women before us fought hard and endured a lot of suffering so that we could get the same jobs as men. If we have to work a little harder so that our future daughters can grow up in a world where their main role model isn't Kim Kardashian, then so be it. Unfair? Yes. But a field with fewer female role models just means that if you succeed, you get to be that much more noteworthy as one of the first women in that position. There's a reason why people know who Marie Curie is while completely forgetting that her husband was actually her lab partner, and that's because you can throw a rock in a chem lab and hit a male scientist but need a microscope to find a female one (science analogies are not so much our thing, but we tried).

THE WAGE GAP

One of the most widely recognized inequalities women face today is unequal pay. The wage gap is a very real thing and is defined as *the difference between median earnings of men and women relative to median earnings of men.* (This sounds confusing, but all it means is that women are generally paid less than men for equivalent jobs.) According to the Economic Policy Institute, as of 2016, the unadjusted pay gap in the United States is about 20 percent, which means that for every dollar men earn, women earn 80 percent of that shit. And that's just for *white* women; the percentage is much worse for women of color. Black and Hispanic women have a wage gap of 65 percent and 56 percent, respectively. When you think about how much money you could save toward a house, your kid's tuition, or one Cartier Love bracelet with that difference, you'll probably be as mad as we are about this.

Plus, note the word *unadjusted* in this scenario. This means that the wage gap doesn't take into account shit like women who may choose to take maternity leave or choose certain jobs or to work fewer hours than others in the same positions. Making these choices may impact your yearly salary for logical reasons, rather than sexist ones. But even when those things are adjusted for, there's still a large pay disparity. We need to figure out how to close it because there is no way we can continue to kill it at work, missing happy hours and girls trips to work our asses off while that lazy bro (the one who ghosted you and wouldn't even take you to that Michelin-starred restaurant) can still skate by making more money than you.

Obviously, there's a ton of legislation that can be passed by the government, and corporate policies that can be enacted by business owners to help close the wage gap by instituting things like mandatory paid maternity leave and by passing wage-equality legislation and ensuring access to affordable childcare. But while you wait for the government to do a solid for 50 percent of the workforce, there's also shit you can work on right from your desk or while passing the time getting a pedicure. Here's what you can do to close the pay gap.

Negotiate till you die: Did you know that only 7 percent of women negotiate their salaries compared to 57 percent of men? If you can negotiate the price of a jacket at the Florence leather market, you can negotiate your fucking yearlong salary. We taught you how to do this in earlier chapters, but this is pivotal if you want to make the same amount of money as men. Take a lesson from Cher Horowitz when she told her dad that grades were just a jumping-off point to start negotiations, and get on it. Not just sporadically. Negotiate or ask if there's more on the table literally every time you're in a conversation about your salary or a potential raise.

Know that you are the shit: Thanks to imposter syndrome, too many women don't think they deserve a certain job or higher pay. Societally, girls have been taught that they'll be rewarded for keeping their mouths shut and taking what's given to them.

Guys don't really have this issue and are taught from a young age that they're amazing and deserve everything and can be anything, so they're a little more equipped to get what they're worth. Being confident in a negotiation means overcoming these doubts, at least to some degree. Everyone knows that negotiating is scary, and even if you truly know that you're the shit deep down, this might call for a little bit of faking it till you make it.

> When I first started The Oprah Show . . . we syndicated, and I have all women producers, five women. . . . I went in and I said, "Everybody needs raises." And the management at the time said, "Why do they need raises? Why do a bunch of girls need raises? They're not married, they don't have children, they don't have their own houses." This was in 1985 in Chicago. . . . I said if you don't give them money, then I'm going to sit down.
>
> —Oprah Winfrey

Talk to your work friends about their salaries: The only way to know if you're getting paid less than men for the same jobs is if you fucking ask. So don't feel weird casually asking Jason in accounting how he can afford that trip to Mykonos every summer while your idea of a vacation is swimming in your grandma's pool. If you find out you're making less than your peers for the same jobs, make like it's the NYC subway system and say something.

A NOTE ON IMPOSTER SYNDROME

You know when you have a pretty great job and everything is seemingly going well but there's still this pit in your stomach that one day someone's going to to catch on that you don't belong? You're afraid that your boss is going to be like, wait, she doesn't actually know shit and is a total fraud. Well, that's imposter syndrome and it's a real psychological phenomenon. We feel that we got to the top by accident, we could fail at any second, and that when anyone congratulates us on our accomplishments, we say we got lucky. The crazy thing about imposter syndrome is that in all likelihood, your boss, and probably your boss's boss, is feeling the exact same thing. So just remember that next time you have doubts about your success.

Pick jobs that have good family policies: If you want to have kids, make sure you're working for a company that cares about their workers and that their female employees are happy. Assuming you have the financial security to pick and choose, be selective about the jobs you take and make sure they work for you.

Speak up for women getting paid well: If you're lucky enough to be a boss or the person determining salaries, encourage the women who work for you to do all the aforementioned shit. Make sure you're compensating and coaching women who look up to you about how to stand up for themselves. And also, actually pay men and women equally in your own company. That's just like, the rules of feminism.

Inspirational Career Betch: Jennifer Lawrence

I'm over trying to find the "adorable" way to state my opinion and still be likable! Fuck that.
—Jennifer Lawrence

In 2016, Jennifer Lawrence was the highest-paid actress in Hollywood. When the Sony hack revealed the amounts that actors and actresses were being paid for movies, it was discovered that JLaw was making a shit ton less than her male costars. Obviously, Jennifer isn't the one suffering most from the wage gap, but what's important is that she used her position of power in the movie industry to talk about how messed up it is. She's the star of the Hunger Games series, which is about a female protagonist taking charge to save the world from a corrupt society, and she knew she had to act like it. In an essay, she wrote about how she wouldn't keep quiet just so she could continue being America's sweetheart and adored by everyone. She stressed that women should negotiate more and let their voices be heard. She noted that men in Hollywood are never afraid of appearing too aggressive or "bratty" while voicing their opinions.

Personally, we've learned that men can truly be the biggest brats of all, especially when they feel slightly inferior or marginalized (welcome to this side of the street, bro). Jen showed us how to use a platform to inspire other women, and also that being liked as a woman doesn't mean you have to shut the fuck up and take whatever is given to you.

FEMINIST TERMS AND HOW TO USE THEM

The three of us have had the pleasure of working primarily with other women as we built our company. So in addition to having a fully stocked pantry full of makeup remover pads and tampons (no tampon tax in the Betches office), we've also been able to bypass a lot of the really annoying shit that men tend to do to keep women down at work. But although our company was built by powerful women (yes, we're talking about ourselves), that doesn't mean we haven't encountered our share of asshole bros along the way.

Thanks to Beyoncé and Chimamanda Ngozi Adichie on "Flawless," we are all familiar with the definition of feminism. Now that modern women have taken it upon ourselves to show everyone that feminism has less to do with burning your bra and man-hating, and more to do with loving yourself and getting the respect you deserve, it's time for you to embrace the term and not get freaked out when somebody asks you point-blank if you're a feminist. The #MeToo movement taught us how powerful it is when brave women come together to speak up. But unfortunately, vocalizing controversial experiences and opinions is neither easy nor safe. Feminism gives us a means to understand the context of the behavior we receive from men who take advantage of us, and understanding feminist terms with confidence can help us navigate inappropriate interactions with men in the workplace and allow us to speak up.

Feminism: A belief in and desire for equality between the sexes. That's literally it. So as long as you think men and women should be treated equally and given the same opportunities, you're a feminist. Don't let some asshole you're dating or any man you work with make you feel like being a feminist means you're a lame, cat-loving spinster who hates men. That definition of feminism, much like your boss's use of the term *on fleek*, is very fucking dead, and it's time for all halfway-decent human beings to self-identify as feminists. Instead, we should call out those who claim *not* to be feminists and ask them why the fuck not.

Gaslighting: So, there are a lot of super-long articles about the psychological impacts of gaslighting and how damaging it is, but for the sake of not boring you, here's a crash course. Remember when your so-called boyfriend blew you off for like, a full week and then told everyone you were a "psycho bitch" when you finally went off on him via text even though he pushed you to it? That's gaslighting. Remember that dude you met on a dating app who said his ex was "crazy" but then after a little investigation you found out he was the one still texting other bitches? Again, that's gaslighting. Remember that time you were in the car with your hot stepbrother and some chick in a beret laughed at your understanding of *Hamlet* even though you know you remember Mel Gibson accurately? You guessed it—gaslighting.

> There was blood coming out of her eyes, blood coming out of her wherever.
>
> —Donald Trump on Megyn Kelly after she had asked him a legitimate question

Gaslighting is a term that comes from some old-ass movie that means when a bro (or anyone, really—women can gaslight too) tries to deflect their own shittiness by trying to make you feel insecure and stupid, usually by telling everyone you're crazy, thereby making you *feel* crazy. Remember when Donald Trump basically said Megyn Kelly was being really mean to him because she was on her period? (Something that apparently is not so insane that it can't get you elected to be the president of the free world.) This is the ultimate in shady bro behavior, but unlike other shady things bros do, it's not attractive. Gaslighting is used by people who want to take away your agency and make you feel small, so next time somebody tries to do it to you, just be like, "You can go gaslight your back now. Bye."

Slut shaming: Slut shaming is when people fail to mind their own fucking business and act like what you do or don't put into your front pocket has anything to do with them. For some betches, "having sex sometimes" means "some of the time" and for others it means "basically every weekend now that I'm on dating apps." Whatever. Do you. A betch is a gift to society, and if she chooses to bestow that gift upon an entire basketball team, that's her prerogative. No judgment. But when some dude you work with tries to bring up something about your or someone else in the office's dating history or sex life to make them feel shitty about themselves, that's particularly toxic slut shaming. Luckily, betches have been longtime champions of the anti-slut-shaming movement by embracing the joys of dressing like a slut (in appropriate situations) and

> *If men got pregnant, you could get an abortion at an ATM.*
>
> —Selina Meyer, *Veep*

always keeping in mind that we've "got to stop calling each other sluts and whores, because it just makes it okay for guys to call you sluts and whores." Thanks, Tina.

Patriarchy: A hierarchical-structured society in which men hold more power. This has existed since pretty much the dawn of time, but thankfully over the years women have been given the tools and role models to take back some of their power.

Bropropriate: This is when a guy steals an idea from a woman and puts it into the world as his own. Like when your manager takes all the PowerPoints you do and pretends he made them or says that all the important insightful shit you said at the meeting was his idea.

Mansplain: This happens when a guy tries to explain shit to you like you're stupid, when in fact you know more about the issue at hand than he does. Remember when you went to a casino with a bro and he tried to explain to you how blackjack works even though you're fucking amazing at blackjack? Remember when you asked about your specific medical benefits and the HR rep gave you a condescending definition of insurance when you didn't fucking ask that? Remember when the Starbucks barista tried to tell you how to pronounce your *own* name? That's mansplaining.

Manterrupting: When a man interrupts a woman, especially excessively, in a way that suggests "forget what this woman has to say and listen to me." Remember when Kanye grabbed Taylor Swift's mic at the 2009 MTV VMAs and decided to let everyone know that he thought Beyoncé should've won? Remember when Donald Trump interrupted Hillary Clinton twenty-two times in the first twenty-six minutes of the 2016 presidential debate? Remember when you were trying to pitch your boss an idea and your male coworker kept interrupting to give his two irrelevant cents? That's manterrupting.

Manspreading: When men take up excess space by sitting with their legs far apart. Remember when there were like, zero seats on the train and some douchebag decided to spread his legs and take up four? Yeah, this doesn't really have anything to do with office politics, but it's really fucking annoying and gross. Stop kidding yourself—you don't need that much space, because your dick is just not that big.

OFFICE ROMANCE/FLIRTING

It's no secret that Americans spend a shit ton of time at work. Statistical fact: anyone with a full-time job sees the people they work with way more than anyone else they know. And as much as we love our friends, families, and dogs, we're not logging forty hours a week locked in the same rooms being forced to interact, socialize, and make important decisions with them all day. This is a good thing, because doing so would probably make you want to murder these people, but it's also a bad thing because you instead want to murder the people you actually work with. Anyway, because we spend so much time with our coworkers, it's only natural that we wind up becoming friends with them. Sometimes, we even wind up having sex with them.

According to Match's *Singles in America* 2015 study, 35 percent of people have dated someone they work with. While this number doesn't exactly tell us if "dating" includes that time you blacked out and hooked up with your cube mate at the office holiday party, it's pretty clear that in the majority of work environments, there are more than a few people at the office who have wound up doing anything from heavily flirting to actually getting married.

Dating someone at work can be exciting! It gives you a reason to put on makeup and actually make an effort. Plus, since we're so busy building our careers these days, going on dates after work often feels like a chore, as if you're adding on another full-time job, thus making the office romance even more appealing. But don't go jumping every cute guy who changes the coffee filter for you. There's a lot more you need to know before you go there with a coworker.

OFFICE GOGGLES

Much like beer goggles, office goggles are when you become attracted to a guy at work who you would never even think about hooking up with in the real world. Your limited access to hot and fun people of the opposite sex has now deemed this dude an actual viable option.

Now that we've established that you can and probably will at some point in your career feel attracted to someone you work with, let's discuss what to do about it.

Generally speaking, office romances are a bad idea. While the phrase "don't shit where you eat" is really fucking disgusting, it's important to remember every time you consider taking things to the next level with a coworker. Think of your worst breakup, with the most annoying, terrible asshole you can imagine. Now think about having to not only *not* throw a drink in this guy's face every time you see him but having to actually interact with him about sales pitches and spreadsheets daily, all while trying to hide from your boss that you had a hookup-gone-very-wrong with your coworker. Not only will you have to deal with this person on a regular basis if things go south, you will also have to deal with having constant inadvertent updates on their life, from overhearing his after-work plans with friends, to potentially knowing other people in the office he may flirt with or date in the future.

Welcome to your worst-case office-romance scenario. You're now in actual hell, and there is no way out unless one of you quits, is fired, or is arrested for strangling the other at the summer offsite.

Even worse than emotionally ruining your work environment, a bad office romance can also fuck up your actual work. How are you supposed to concentrate on crafting the perfect tweet if you're stalking Jason in the kitchen or crying in the bathroom because he walked past your desk without even saying hello this morning? The office has enough politics without having to navigate using a sick day to avoid seeing your ex on Valentine's Day.

So yes, dating a coworker is the worst idea since you realized that your face shape doesn't work with bangs *after* getting bangs. But just like that time you cost your parents $3,000 by going over your family's data plan in Cancún, shit happens. If you can't resist dating someone at work, we're going to give you the nine unofficial rules for dating a coworker without having to burn your office to the ground.

> **Holly:** So we kiss occasionally.
>
> **Oscar:** Not occasionally. All the time.
>
> **Phyllis:** Yeah, and it's not just the kissing. It's the flirtatious whispering.
>
> **Stanley:** The flirtatious tickling.
>
> **Michael:** Whispering and tickling have their place in business.
>
> —The Office

1. *Despacito* (**Take it slow**): Hang out outside the office as friends to see if his personality outside of work is just as good as his office personality. Maybe Eric's hyperorganized ambitious tendencies are sexy in sales meetings but not sexy when he screams at you for spilling wine on his couch.

2. **Keep it quiet:** Don't start posting Instagram stories of your date nights and sending email blasts about how you and Matt are hooking up. This will not only be embarrassing when things fall apart, but it's important to remember that no one really gives a shit about your relationship unless it concerns them. Since in this stage, this is probably not an established "thing" yet, be cool.

3. **Know your company's dating policy:** Your employee handbook should have some shit in it about office romances, the company policies about disclosing them, and if it's even allowed. Also, read the room. If there are a lot of people who hook up with each other at your job, it's probably more socially acceptable than if the last time anyone got laid in your office was before you were born.

4. **Make sure it's legal:** Make sure the person you're dating isn't your direct superior or report. If it is, there's a ton

of potential legal issues and anything you say or don't say could be taken as someone being given preferential treatment because you're sleeping with them. This could open you up to a lawsuit and/or general weirdness. Example: During that *Friends* episode when Rachel tells everyone her assistant Tag, who is unqualified, is gay so that she can continue to keep him as a viable dating option for herself. Highly inappropriate, Rachel!

5. Decide together when to disclose your relationship: Don't go telling anyone at work (especially your respective bosses) about the fact that you're dating without talking to him first. If you guys really have something that you want to pursue, talk to him about when you're going to tell people and make a game plan in case things don't work out. It goes without saying that you shouldn't be making out in the supply closet, but go above and beyond

> *Jan Levinson (on submitting to HR that she's dating Michael):* I am taking a calculated risk. What's the upside? I overcome my nausea, fall deeply in love, babies, normalcy, no more self-loathing. Downside? I, uh, date Michael Scott publicly and collapse in on myself like a dying star.
>
> —The Office

this obvious rule by creating an extra amount of distance between the two of you at work. No need to suggest to your manager that you two partner on something work-related and make shit even more complicated than it has to be.

6. **Be low-key:** Don't make anyone at work feel uncomfortable by talking about your amazing sex or the next trip you guys have planned. Don't email a picture of your boyfriend half naked at Sandals Jamaica to your office Slack channel. Don't tell people about your relationship problems. Not only will everyone find you annoying, this will create a shit ton of office gossip that will be very entertaining for everyone else while very awkward and embarrassing for you. See rule number two, no one gives a shit.

7. **Don't fight at work, idiot:** Do not take this year's budget meeting as an excuse to call Matt out on the fact that he cheaped out on your birthday gift. This isn't *Vanderpump Rules*, and you're not being paid to start drama at work. The best way to not let dating someone at work interfere with your work is to act as though you're not dating this person at work. So complete your tasks and don't spend work hours googling tantric sex classes for the two of you or messaging him on Slack about your mom's birthday brunch.

8. **Triple-check the texts and emails you're sending:** See: Rachel's fake performance evaluation for Tag that

says he's a great kisser and that she likes his "teeny-tiny tushy," which was accidentally submitted to HR. Now that we think about it, how did Rachel get away with this shit?

9. Think about what you'll do if things *do* work out: In the extremely rare scenario that you wind up marrying this person and things actually work out, one of you should probably leave the company. The stronger your relationship is, the more it'll affect your job environment. Plus, who wants to spend all day at work with someone they're married to? It may have worked for Jim and Pam, but that's just because they took all the tension and aggression in their lives out on Dwight.

Bottom line: when it comes to your career and dating, make a point to keep those two worlds as separate as possible. Despite how chill TV and movies make dating coworkers seem, things can unravel, and you could wind up fucking yourself over. This isn't *Mad Men*, and you aren't Don's second wife, Megan. Don't be the girl who seems like she's only there to meet her husband or hook up. Doing that will make you seem like you don't take your job seriously and will undermine any efforts you actually do put in at work.

If you do meet someone you connect with at work, be smart about it. Your office isn't a sorority mixer, it's a business where people go to earn a living. Respect that, and your co-workers will respect you.

SEXUAL HARASSMENT

So like, what's the difference between dating a coworker and sexual harassment?

The aforementioned examples of office romances assume the relationships being discussed are two-sided and consensual. Sexual harassment is what happens when this isn't the case or when someone uses their position or power to coerce you into sexual interaction with them, or makes you uncomfortable with obscene remarks.

There can be a fine line between what might be considered friendly and platonic banter and sexual harassment. Like, it's hard to create a hard rule for discerning whether your boss's compliment that you "could be a part-time model" is meant in a pervy way or just a really accurate statement. Not that people should be commenting on your appearance at work, but use your judgment. Basically, if you feel like someone is making repeated unwanted comments or lays their hands on you in any uninvited way, you're being sexually harassed.

Here are some examples of what's okay versus not okay when it comes to interactions at work.

Okay	Not Okay
Your boss gives you a gift certificate for a massage to reward your long hours.	Your boss gives you a personal massage as he passes your desk to reward your long hours.
Your boss texts you to tell you that you did a great job during your presentation.	Your boss texts you to tell you that your ass looked great during your presentation.
Your boss introduces you to his wife and kids at a work social event.	Your boss introduces you to his boner at a work social event.
Your manager tells you you're a little off your game today.	Your manager tells you that you might want to put on more makeup today.
Your manager complains that he hasn't had time to watch his favorite shows in a while.	Your manager complains that he hasn't had sex in a while.

Until relatively recently, most women didn't say anything about pervasive sexual harassment because, if they did, they were vilified for causing problems. Most sexual harassment claims were swept under the rug. As we discussed earlier in this chapter, women haven't been in the workforce that long, and that's definitely one of the factors that has led to the absence of strict rules about sexual harassment and the chill attitude that a lot of powerful men have had about how women deserve to be treated in work settings. If the Harvey Weinstein situation has taught us anything though, it's that time is definitely fucking up for men who think they can make unwanted sexual passes at whoever they want.

So like, why are these guys so obsessed with harassing women?

Sexual harassment is not about sex; it's about power. According to Neil Malamuth, a professor of psychology and communication at UCLA, men who harass or assault women often have a combination of two shitty personality characteristics: "hostile masculinity" and "impersonal sexuality." These traits then become amplified by power.

Men with "hostile masculinity" essentially get hard from having power over women. Most of the time they're men who betches wouldn't have looked twice at in high school and now have some complex about how their ability to have sex with women defines their personal worth. Not shockingly, these guys are usually narcissists. A lot of times these types of men will use money to try to attract women and appear fuck-worthy.

Men with "impersonal sexuality" want to have sex without

intimacy, so don't expect them to be snugglers. This person probs didn't get enough love as a child and has major intimacy issues. Unfortunately, their coworkers now have to deal with this in the form of sexual harassment.

And one trait that wasn't covered in Malamuth's research but that we think is super important is just plain sexism/misogyny. Most of the men making headlines for sexual harassment have really sexist attitudes in every aspect of their lives, even if it's secretive. They're the types to make fun of the Women's March, make jokes about women being in the kitchen, and lose their hard-ons when they find out you make more money than them. And even if a guy is paying lip service to feminism, keep an eye out for how he really behaves around powerful (and not powerful) women.

What do I do if I'm being sexually harassed?

Simple. If you're being sexually harassed, you need to speak up. Sometimes women hesitate because they're so uncomfortable that they want to leave their jobs regardless and don't think it's worth it. Other times, it's because they're afraid of the backlash or of being called too sensitive. Sometimes, it's because their boss is a big fucking deal and they don't feel like anyone will believe them or that the harasser is too important to the company to actually be held responsible for his actions.

A lot of the time, though, it's because they don't have proper documentation. It's hard to conclusively prove that your superior told you multiple times while drunk how much he wants to fuck you. Not every obscene comment is made in writing or in public; it can be scary for women to pit their word against a man's. So pretend the situation is a very important meeting and write that shit down.

First, familiarize yourself with your workplace sexual harassment rules. Some companies are stricter than others and/ or have clear policies involving what is and what isn't acceptable. For example, if you work at Facebook, you're allowed to ask someone out one time. If they say no, you can't ask again. That's just like, the rules of sexual harassment. If you say, "I can't that night" or "I'm busy," that also counts as a no. Leave it to Mark Zuckerberg, the inventor of FaceMash, to be extremely aware of how you might make up a bullshit excuse to get out of awkwardly rejecting a date from someone you sit next to every day.

We looked everywhere (Google) for what to do if you think you may be experiencing sexual harassment, and here's what we found. In a 2016 interview with *Forbes*, Donna Ballman, employment lawyer and author of *Stand Up for Yourself Without Getting Fired*, offered steps you should take if you believe you're being sexually harassed.

We broke them down for you.

1. **Document any quid pro quo:** *Quid pro quo* is a fancy-ass Latin term meaning "exchange." Basically, you should document (a.k.a. write down) anytime someone tries to offer you a job, a promotion, or any special favors in return for something sexual or threatens to discipline or fire you if you don't give them sexual favors. Like when Salma Hayek said that Harvey Weinstein threatened to not release her movie *Frida* in theaters when she wouldn't return his sexual advances. Write down the time, place, and any witnesses of the exchange. And it's okay if you don't have witnesses, write that shit down anyway.

2. **Document any comments or different treatment you receive:** The second type of sexual harassment is called "hostile environment," and it's more common than quid pro quo. This happens when you're being harassed because of your gender but it's not always an outright exchange. That's like if your boss says that women are dumber than men or says anything to the effect of how

> **Brick** (opposing women in the newsroom): I read somewhere that their periods attract bears. Bears can smell the menstruation.
>
> **Brian:** Well, that's just great. You hear that, Ed? Bears. Now you're putting the whole station in jeopardy.
>
> —Anchorman

you as a woman would do a shittier job on a certain project

than a man would, or that you shouldn't be allowed into a certain meeting because you're a woman. Making filthy "jokes" to make you uncomfortable, or commenting inappropriately on your body also fall into this category. Again, write it down and timestamp it.

3. **Safeguard your notes:** Now that you have it all written down, don't keep said notes at work. Keep all your documentation on your home computer or personal phone and out of the office entirely. If you're fired while you're pursuing action, you won't have access to your work computer and then you'll lose all your evidence, fucking duh.

4. **Save everything:** Make like you're in a scandalous group text and take fucking screenshots. Save physical cards and notes, print inappropriate emails, even commit the highest offense of all: screenshot your Snapchats. Don't let that dick pic from your manager get lost in cyberspace because you were too traumatized to take a screenshot in under ten seconds. That's how court cases are lost.

5. **File a report:** This is like, the most important thing you can do. According to Ballman, the Supreme Court (ever heard of it?) says you can only sue if you have documented

evidence of reporting sexual harassment. And by reporting, we don't mean to your friend group at brunch. Report
what's going on to your HR representative and then, after
you report it, follow up with an email reiterating what you
just reported and that you appreciate them looking into
this immediately. It's literally their job to make it stop after
you've reported it, and if they don't, report it again. If you're
retaliated against, report that, too. Unlike a triple text, a
triple report will save you from having a mental breakdown
when you're in the midst of getting this asshole fired.

6. **File a complaint with the Equal Employment Opportunity Commission (EEOC):** If your employer
doesn't do jack shit after you've reported it to them, it's
time to go outside your workplace and report the offenses
to the EEOC and potentially sue the shit out of your
company.

7. **Lawyer up:** Even if you're not sure you have a case, you
should ask an employment lawyer. A lot of people offer
these services pro bono or will at least take your phone
call for free. Depending on what the lawyer says, you could
potentially sue for a lot of money and like, never have to
work again.

8. **GTFO:** Start looking for another job, even while you're documenting your harassment. If you don't feel safe or feel like your environment is abusive, it's time to get the hell out of there. You can still build a case if you leave, and you'll also help prevent other women from getting harassed by letting your company know that there are consequences and shit.

The bottom line is that no one should have to feel uncomfortable at work and there are things that you can do about it. Your company has a legal obligation to protect you from sexual harassment. Take a page from Inspirational Betch Elle Woods's character and let your employers know that while you may be hot, that doesn't mean that you don't deserve just as much respect as everyone else.

TL;DR

The ways that men and women have interacted in the workplace and what's expected of them have changed dramatically over the last century. Hopefully in time and with enough education, women and men will be essentially equal in the workforce, be it reflected in their salaries, the respect they're given, and in what is expected of them as humans and contributors in their careers.

It's up to all of us to call out bullshit when we see it so that things can change. It's also up to us to learn how to negotiate and stand up for ourselves at the same rate as men do. After all, our forebetches didn't fight for the right to be able to buy their own two-bedroom apartments so that we could spend our days dodging sexts from our managers while getting paid less than them.

> **Bobbie Barrett** (to Peggy): You're never gonna get that corner office until you start treating Don as an equal. And no one will tell you this, but you can't be a man. Don't even try. Be a woman. Powerful business when done correctly.
>
> —Mad Men

Dear Betches,

I have a few questions about work relationships and how to navigate them. Two months ago, my boyfriend of two years broke up with me. I was pretty upset at first but have started the process of moving on—sleeping and dating around. I work at a really small office of eight people, so everyone pretty much knows my business and knows I've been casually dating/sleeping around.

There's one guy at work who I'm pretty flirty with and have a major crush on. My other coworkers really want us to get together and have even told me that he likes me. When we go out for drinks we tend to get handsy with each other.

My question would be, how do I handle this situation? I'm definitely not ready for anything super serious (at the moment), but I do like him and think there could be something real there down the line. How do I convey my intentions with him are more serious than these other guys I've been dating? Is it totally stupid to start a relationship with a coworker? Especially in a small office like mine?

Sincerely,
I Should Just Work from Home

Dear Work from Home,

We get the temptation to start an office romance. Work is boring, and it's way more exciting to drag yourself out of bed in the morning if there's a cute guy in the office who you're excited to see and flirt with. That being said, tread carefully. Your office only has eight people working in it. That means you and said guy are 25 percent of your office. Let's play this out in a few different scenarios.

Scenario 1: You confess your feelings to said guy, make an awkward attempt to relay the fact that you're down to do more than just hook up, or make a move on him, and he's not interested. So you feel awkward and have to see him every day indefinitely. You try to be cool, but you've been rejected and are hurt and insulted. Say you feel weird about having to see him and also feel ashamed

about sharing information about your personal life at work since you fear that might be the reason he's not interested.

Scenario 2: You confess said feelings and he is down. You hook up, have a great time, even go on a few dates, but things end badly. Now you have to see him every day, listen to office gossip about him seeing other girls, and collaborate daily with the person who broke your heart without running to the bathroom to sob.

Scenario 3: You two hit it off, get married, coparent a miniature goldendoodle, and carpool to work every day. Your home life and your work life are now conjoined and you don't know where one ends and the other begins. You start yelling at him in the break room about the fact that he forgot to pick up the dry-cleaning, causing a scene and getting reprimanded by your boss.

Bottom line, you need to ask yourself if this is really worth the risk of feeling awkward at work if this doesn't work out. You yourself said you're not ready for anything serious, so why risk making everyone in your office uncomfortable for what is probably going to turn out to be a fling? If you're feeling lonely, ask your coworkers to set you up with people who don't work in your office.

That said, if you truly believe this guy is the Jim to your Pam, take it slow. People often find new jobs and don't stay at their current positions for too long. Maintain a friendship and then when one of you inevitably leaves for a new job, confess your feelings. That way you have nothing to lose, and, worst case, it's just your run-of-the-mill disastrous relationship, not a soul-crushing daily run-in with someone you kind of like because there's no one else enticing around to talk to.

Remind yourself that you're just looking to have fun and that the cons definitely outweigh the pros on this one. It's all fun and games until you're Instagram stalking his new girlfriend while he sits at the cubicle next to you.

Sincerely,
Betches

9.
I AM CURRENTLY OUT OF OFFICE

Work-Life Balance

Work-life balance is one of those things everyone talks about but few people actually achieve. We're pretty sure that spending eight-plus hours of your sixteen waking hours every day, when the standard workweek is five out of seven days a week, means that work and "life" can never really be in true balance. Especially not in major cities, where the commute shaves extra hours off the "life" part of your balance. Blame capitalism and the American dream for deluding people into thinking this is possible, but it's not.

Ever notice how the huge corporations who advertise their

amazing policies and benefits that are meant to promote work-life balance are also the same companies where the unspoken expectation is that you're available by email all the time? If anything, the bullshit promotion of work-life balance has actually just become a ploy for your employer to overtake your whole life and ensure that all your time belongs to them, not just the hours you're physically in the office. Sure, they'll let you "work from home whenever you want." What they don't tell you is that this is not actually possible, as you most likely have in-person obligations that prevent you from realistically taking advantage of that policy. You might have a boss who values face time over results, or even if they don't care about how much time you spend at the office, they definitely notice and may decide to use it against you in the court of annual performance reviews.

Whatever it is, we dare you to try using your pursuit of a proper work-life balance as an excuse to leave at 3:00 p.m. on a Wednesday and see how far that gets you. Trust us, no one looks at that person and thinks, *Wow, what an amazing employee, so balanced.* If you need further proof, just note how there's no category for "amazing at work-life balance" on a performance review.

We live in a corporate world in which, even if a company claims to value work-life balance, it often comes at the expense of your advancement because the workload they're giving you prevents you from actually taking advantage of their allegedly chill policies. Just like a Realtor stages a house before trying to sell it to you, those policies exist to get people in the door. But once you're in, you'll notice that work-life balance is about as realistic as the giant Restoration Hardware cloud couch becoming actual property of your future home. Best to be internally pissed about this injustice until you find someone you can discuss it with at Burning Man. As business owners ourselves, we see firsthand how the nature of competition between businesses makes it pretty much impossible for any business to thrive while also creating a truly chill work environment. Sad!

So if there's no such thing as work-life balance, how are you supposed to stay sane when you have people constantly asking you to circle back? Unfortunately, that is entirely up to you and how you choose to manage your life, the type of job you try to get, and the coping mechanisms you put in place to manage stress. In this chapter, we're going to attempt to show you how to create the closest thing possible to a legit work-life balance by showing you how to make the most of life outside of work.

REDEFINING WORK-LIFE BALANCE: NO MORE DELUSIONS

Like any good therapist will tell you, the first thing you need is to undo the damage from all the bullshit in your daily-inspiration emails. Acceptance is the first step. There's no such thing as work-life balance, so if you're expecting to achieve a fifty-fifty life like you read about in some nonsense article, think again. The change needs to happen internally, and most of it has to do with changing your perspective and expectations. Your boss is not suddenly going to start caring that you want to spend more time with your kids or your husband if it affects your productivity. The key is to navigate between your personal and workplace priorities.

First, just accept that achieving balance means that you're going to be off-balance most of the time. Picture one of those old-fashioned scales from the doctor's office or a playground seesaw (for the working moms in the back who are trying to sneak out to pick up their kids from soccer. We see you, moms). One side is always above the other, or if they're ever totally equal, that lasts for about two seconds. The "balance" happens when the two sides are switching places in an equal way. Yes, we know that the work side is going to be weighed down five days a week by default, and there's pretty much nothing you can do about that. The way to deal is to create such a heavy "life" in your off hours that you can come close to the balance promised by your company's recruitment materials.

Before we get to the "life" part of the balance, it's important to figure out how to create a work style that gives you as much free time as possible to live that life. Finding ways to be more organized, prioritize tasks and focus better, and generally become more efficient are really important when figuring out how to get better at your job. The secret is that doing so will also free up extra time that you can spend *not working*, which is both more enjoyable for you and will make you better at your job. It's like a ~~vicious~~ extremely relaxing cycle.

GET YOUR SHIT TOGETHER: HOW TO ORGANIZE AND PRIORITIZE AT WORK

Seriously, once you enter your first real job, it becomes completely unacceptable to not know how to organize yourself and manage your time and tasks. Lack of organization leads to forgetting things, and if you think you can keep track of everything in your head, or that your job involves only one task, you're wrong. The human brain is only capable of remembering like, fifteen things max at any given time, and considering how much molly you did while studying abroad, that number is probably even lower.

Get a fucking notebook and figure out which specific method of information tracking works best for you. Don't be the adult equivalent of the kid whose Trapper Keeper notebook is overflowing with (gasp) non-hole-punched papers and no dividers. If you're a "creative" type and think you're above this type of formalization of your life, that's fine as long as you don't consistently forget things. But realistically, most people—even "creatives"—forget things without some sort of system in place. We have a few ideas that have helped us in the past, but this is by no means an exhaustive list. If you're already a compulsive organizer with the perfect system, feel free to add "ignore us" to your to-do list and then cross it out immediately.

To-do lists: Lists are extremely cathartic because you get to cross shit off them, even if that item is literally *showering* or *call Grandma*. (JK, we know that second one can be more daunting than actual work.) To-do lists keep you from forgetting things from day to day, and your life suddenly seems less stressful after you write it all down because it's no longer your brain's responsibility to remember everything—it's now your notebook's. Lists also make you feel and look productive, even if you never accomplish anything on them. Plus, the feeling when you cross something out, even if you faked it a little, is equivalent to Leonardo DiCaprio's character on quaaludes in *The Wolf of Wall Street*.

Time blocking: Time blocking is a scheduling method where you basically write down what you're going to be doing at every single hour of the day, including scrolling through

Instagram and watching Netflix. Think of it like logging all your calories on a diet. You'll be more aware of what you're actually doing with your time, much like that annoying task makes you hyperaware of all the shit you're stress eating at 10:00 p.m. The idea is that if you know what you plan to be doing, even leisure things, at all times, you won't waste time trying to figure out what to do or stressing about what you "should" be doing. This method also shows you how much free time you actually have, even when you feel like you're like, *soooo busy.* Time blocking definitely works if you stay on top of it, but it's more useful for those with extreme OCD, since technically you should even be time-blocking the time that you'll be writing down the time blocking. It's not for everyone, particularly people who hate rigidity and structure, even though they're probably the ones who need it most.

Phone and calendar reminders: Sure, keep telling yourself you'll definitely remember to post that scheduled instagram for your job, even though you know you plan to be at happy hour at that time. Three pomegranate margaritas later, you get the text from your client, *Where is my post?!* To avoid finding yourself in this position, just set a reminder on your phone, and it will literally . . . remind you. Potential drinks with your friend? Put it in the cal. Need five minutes to write a terrible review of your last Uber driver? Put it in the cal. It's sort of like inviting yourself to have meetings with yourself. This method seems lame AF, but it works. There is literally zero point in relying on your memory when Steve Jobs can just nag you to get things done via incessant notifications.

Carve out email time: Emails are literally never going to stop, and if you're one of those people who likes to maintain inbox zero, chances are that you're going to spend a lot of your day deleting emails rather than doing actual projects. Yes, we know anxiety floods your body when you see your full inbox after a long phoneless meeting (*How the fuck do I get forty-seven emails in the span of one meeting?*), but the truth is that the vast majority of emails can wait. Half of them are automated sales emails, another quarter of them are calendar invites. That leaves just the real emails to respond to, which shouldn't take that long and are rarely that urgent. Some super-productive people recommend blocking out one or two specific times every day to answer emails. We recommend trying it, because sometimes making people sweat it out is fun.

Keep your physical space organized: Studies have shown that looking at a disorganized space makes you more anxious and less personally organized. If this doesn't apply to you, feel free to keep your apartment looking like shit and your desk overflowing with hoardery items. Your call. But everyone knows the feeling of extreme relief and put-togetherness when you finish organizing your closet or cleaning your house. Imagine if you could feel that way all the time, just by keeping things organized regularly. Also, the more you maintain organization, the fewer big cleanups you'll have to do.

If you think you don't have time for maintaining that and tend to let your space deteriorate (don't worry, literally everyone has the pile-of-shit chair), it's probably because you're so stressed out from looking at your self-created mess that you feel that way. Clean that shit up, no one wants to look at a desk that resembles your college bedroom. Don't you feel better already?

> *People cannot change their habits without first changing their way of thinking.*
>
> —Marie Kondo,
> *The Life-Changing Magic of Tidying Up*

Now that this list of tips has made you more type A than Monica Geller, it's important to tackle an even more important strategy, which is figuring out how to prioritize.

PRIORITIZING: SO YOUR BOSS DOESN'T HAVE TO CONSTANTLY ASK YOU FOR SHIT

Figuring out how to prioritize tasks is one of the basic and important skills to have, but there's no golden rule that applies to every job in terms of which tasks should come first. Much like the appropriate time to leave the office and how drunk you can get at happy hour, the priorities vary from job to job, mostly depending on the priorities of the business as a whole.

As managers, one of our biggest annoyances is when an employee doesn't understand the bigger picture of what we're all doing every day and how their individual job fits in. You're not at work to do what you want to do, you're there to do what's necessary, and part of the learning curve of any new position is figuring that out without your boss having to constantly spell out what you should be doing and when. That's why you have a brain and a work wife.

We will gladly answer questions about what's most important for *your* job via DM at a rate of $1,000/hour, but for the purchase price of this book, we can make a general recommendation. It's called the Urgent-Important scale, and we once read about it in one of those v famous self-help books, *The 7 Habits of Highly Effective People*. For the sake of this book, we're going to call it the "Right Fucking Now/Who Fucking Cares" scale. It's extremely simple and will change your life.

Picture a chart with four boxes—actually, you don't even have to picture it, because we're going to draw it for you:

WHO FUCKING CARES ⟶

RIGHT FUCKING NOW ⟶

DO THIS SECOND	DO THIS FIRST
RIGHT FUCKING NOW, NO ONE FUCKING CARES	RIGHT FUCKING NOW. EVERYONE FUCKING CARES
DO THIS LAST	DO THIS THIRD
IT CAN WAIT, NO ONE FUCKING CARES	IT CAN WAIT, EVERYONE FUCKING CARES

On the top two squares of the chart you have the Right Fucking Now items, which is basically how soon you need this thing to be done. Things that go in the top half of the chart include deadlines that are about to pass, preparation for meetings that are about to happen, emails from extremely important people that warrant an immediate response. These are the tasks for which timing matters, and the time is right fucking now.

On the bottom of the chart you have the Who Fucking Cares items, which indicates the importance of the task, how seriously you should take it, and how much effort you should put into it. The right half of the chart, where everybody fucking cares, includes things like big presentations, public- or audience-facing initiatives, major projects, anything involving clients, financial or other reports where mistakes can be extremely problematic, anything that could involve legal jeopardy, etc. A good way to judge the importance of something is to ask yourself how much your performance on that task your boss will consider when thinking about promoting you or giving you a raise. These are central to your company's business and/or revenue. Or, if you're not a revenue-generating person, it's the thing of which the quality directly reflects on your overall performance.

The way to use this chart is to look at your to-do list and assign each task to a box. Then, start doing them. Temptingly, the tasks in the lower-left corner usually take the least time and it feels more amazing to cross things off your to-do list than it does to semi-tackle a small piece of a big, annoying project that you can't immediately get out of the way. We know, we're compulsive to-do listers, too (at least Sami and Aleen are).

But like any sober person will tell you, it's not about getting your next fix. It's about getting shit done in the right way at the right time so you don't show up to the content meeting without having properly brainstormed the requested number of Kylie Jenner–related headlines (depending on where you work, this would probably fall into the Right Fucking Now/ Nobody Fucking Cares box, because you need to have it done before the meeting, but it probably won't get you fired if you don't do it that well).

Once you have your work priorities in order and have taken care of a few of them, it's obviously time to take a break and relax. The secret to creating a really effective work-life balance is to understand that not all breaks are created equal; if you spend your weekends recovering from binge-drinking episodes, you probably won't come back to work on Monday feeling that refreshed and balanced. Absolutely no judgment on that but like, just don't still be hungover on Monday. If you want to make your weekends more refreshing but, let's face it, also more lame, we now take you to a discussion of one of our favorite topics, self-care.

SELF-CARE: IT'S NOT JUST FOR WELLNESS INFLUENCERS

Everyone is different (*OMG, so insightful, Betches, how do you come up with this?!*), and we all have different motivations that make us tick, for good or bad. Probably the biggest trick to success at work-life balance is figuring out what works for you and ignoring all the other annoying advice that doesn't align with that.

A lot of photos have been captioned hailing the importance of self-care, mostly beneath highly filtered photos of people taking a break from frothing matcha to take a bath filled with rose petals and blood-orange slices. But if you're anything like us and don't have time or desire to milk your own almonds, you'll agree that this faux-inspiration isn't actually helpful. If anything, living up to Instagram's definition of self-care just causes more stress and bank-account depletion.

True self-care is not glamorous or photogenic, the same way that working out is not the same as sharing your new Lululemon sports bra in an Equinox-mirror selfie. In fact, anything that involves taking a selfie is the opposite of self-care, and even if what you're doing could legitimately be considered self-care, the fact that you're documenting it for public consumption is automatically destroying a great deal of the benefit from the activity.

As for what activities actually constitute self-care, this is what's different for everyone and why we say that you have to figure out what it means to you. According to the allegedly reputable *Merriam-Webster*, it is defined as "care for the self," which sounds like someone didn't even feel like pretending to do the assignment. Really, the term just means doing something enjoyable that relaxes and satisfies you so that you can feel recharged and more energetic later on. Some examples of things we think can legitimately de-stress you are:

- Meditating, as long as you don't brag about it after.
- Making to-do lists, particularly the part where you add things you've already done for the sake of crossing them off.
- Working out, as long as you don't brag about it after.
- Cooking, but not for the sake of instagramming it or binge eating.
- Reading an actual book for fun.
- Listening to music.
- Watching your fave TV show while not compulsively picking up your phone every two seconds to look at Instagram.
- Napping.
- Getting a drink with a friend, but like, an actual friend, not the one you canceled on three times due to social anxiety before finally following through on the plans.
- Playing with your pet, without a phone between you and the dog's face.
- Actually enjoying a call with someone in your family (sounds crazy, but it's possible, if you're not trying to get off the phone with them the entire time).
- Doing a puzzle or knitting, if you're a grandma at heart.
- Lighting a candle, not instagramming it.
- Just getting the fuck off your phone.

You'll notice that only one entry on this list involves a screen, and nothing here involves social media or scrolling mindlessly on your phone, which brings us to the biggest piece of self-care and work-life balance: Get the fuck off your phone.

GET THE FUCK OFF YOUR PHONE

We know, it's weird that three girls who constantly refresh Instagram are preaching the importance of unplugging. We're not saying it's easy, but the three times we've actually tried it, it made a huge difference. Every time you receive a notification, your brain releases serotonin, which is pretty much a mild form of doing a line of coke, making your phone extremely addictive. That twitch of withdrawal you start to get when you haven't checked your phone in a while is literally a chemical reaction in your brain, not just your genuine curiosity about Kim Kardashian's latest nude mirror pic.

But, Betches, my whole life is on my phone! Yeah, we know, we have phones, too. We're not saying you can't use your phone for utility, we're just recommending that you spend some time off social media and your email. Trust us, the thirst-trap instagrams will be there when you get back, as will the annoying emails from your colleagues. If you happen to miss the weekend Slack thread about the curvature of your company's new logo, we have a feeling you'll survive and no promotions will be lost over it. We're not advocating that you spend *a lot* of time off your phone, just that you build in breaks in order to prevent burnout.

But my boss hates when I miss emails! Pretty sure your boss can wait until the end of *The Bachelor* for a reply; she's not going to die because you decided to have a phoneless dinner without turning on your vacation responder. You're entitled to have some unplugged time, especially at times when you know you're not expected to be doing anything specific and you've fulfilled all your responsibilities. If it becomes an issue, you should respectfully explain that you try to take time to unplug at night or on the weekends so that you can be more efficient and better at your job during standard work hours. Assuming you're a pretty good employee and on top of things in general, this explanation will be understood by most rational and nonworkaholic assholes.

Not only are you entitled to be off your phone, but getting off your phone gives you time to do all the aforementioned self-care activities without distraction. It's honestly hard to really appreciate a book and get the benefit of reading it when you're checking your texts every three minutes. *No*, he didn't text you back, and it would probably benefit you to wait longer to respond regardless. Even though *you* know you don't have a life, that doesn't mean everyone else has to know.

Another time we highly recommend getting the fuck off your phone (and in particular off your email) is when you're on vacation. We've all worked with someone who goes on vacation yet is constantly in contact with their colleagues. Is this black-sand beach so boring that you'd rather be updating a sales report over your Google Sheets app? Assuming you're not the owner of your business, and even if you feel extremely passionate about what you're doing, we personally can't see why you'd want to waste your vacation days like that, and also, stop emailing us. Your vacation is also your coworkers' vacation from *you*. When you give your coworkers a break from you, they'll probably forget about that tuna melt you once reheated in the office microwave and will forgive you while you're gone. Everyone wins.

Even if it *is* your own business and you feel a need to constantly be on top of things, the secret about unplugging is that when you do it, you come back much more motivated and efficient without even realizing it. Think you're too in demand for that? You know Shonda Rhimes? One of the most successful showrunners and producers in what is perhaps the most stereotypically white and male professions around? Turns out Shonda instituted a no-work-email-at-night-or-weekends policy that she's extremely strict about. If one of the most prolific production companies of our time can function without that

9:00 p.m. email, we think your colleagues can live without your little *Sounds good!* reply. True, firing off a quick response makes you feel devoted, but that doesn't take into account the negative impact of constantly being on your phone all the time and how that wears you down and burns you out in the long run.

The bottom line is that "always working" actually means "always working not as well as you would if you would chill the fuck out for ten minutes."

YOU'RE OFF YOUR PHONE, NOW WHAT? GET A HOBBY.

We already gave you a list of things that can replace screen time, but what's the point of it? The point is that other activities give you a release from the constant stimulation of having notifications firing for forty-five different apps at a time. They give you a chance to involve yourself in the things that actually promote mental health rather than further your decline into an app-swiping robot with no ability to interact with the human race IRL.

Hobbies are not only beneficial to your sanity, they're actually beneficial to your career, because whether we like it or not, it's not really possible to hide behind a screen all day.

Sure, the most successful people spend a lot of time on their email, but being "really good at emailing" is probably not what got them to where they are today.

More likely, the most successful people you know were highly competent, creative, *and* well-liked and trusted by peers, bosses, and the people they managed. None of those things will ever be achieved by adding extra exclamation points to your *Hope you had a nice weekend!* email openers.

Being well-liked involves face time, relating to people in a genuine way, and having ideas and shit to talk about besides work. If you don't do anything outside of work and spend all your free time in scrolling spirals, the chances that you have anything to talk about aside from which fashion bloggers are currently pregnant are very small. And that makes you boring.

We recommend taking at least some portion of your weekend and devoting it to an activity that doesn't involve focusing on social media, your phone, or anything digital. See an actual movie, do something outdoors, try a new experience, cook some shit. That way you not only get the benefit of the actual activity but you have a legitimate answer to the obligatory "Do anything interesting this weekend?" question you'll inevitably be asked most, if not all, Monday mornings for the rest of your career.

THE WORKFORCE ESCAPE HATCH:
MOTHERHOOD AND MATERNITY LEAVE

A disclaimer: none of us happen to be mothers as of now, nor do we have motherhood in our near future (at least not in the next nine months). Our closest brushes with motherhood during our adult lives are basically having had employees go on maternity leave, seeing friends or siblings with babies, observing our own working mothers, and the things we read on the internet. While we may not be experts, we're definitely aware that a nearly silent social war is being waged between stay-at-home moms, working moms, and non-moms. Amy Poehler literally has an entire section of her book *Yes Please* dedicated to the conflict and judgment slung at each of the groups by the others, and TBH, it makes us feel a little relieved that we don't have to deal with it yet. Judgment from other people is probably the last thing you need when you're trying to advance in your career or like, figure out how the whole breastfeeding thing works.

Women who want to be mothers are criticized as not being "feminist" enough, while women who want to pursue high-powered careers are criticized as either neglecting their children or not caring about babies/being maternal enough or some BS like that. Women who want both aren't able to devote enough time to either, and how dare you neglect your career/baby/feminist principles. It's almost like no one cares about allowing women to make their own choices about how to run their lives without having to answer to a thousand unsolicited opinions. Oh, wait . . .

We're strong believers that every situation is unique and people should just do whatever the fuck makes them happy. If you're extremely driven toward career achievement and enjoy sleeping through the night more than shopping for cute little Ralph Lauren baby booties, then it might be for the best that you choose to have kids later in life or not at all. If you find work extremely boring and don't see yourself going anywhere with it but feel your uterus about to burst every time you see an UPPA baby stroller, then maybe career advancement isn't going to be your thing (if you can afford to opt out). If you feel a pull toward both, then you might be able to figure out how to make it work while fending off criticism from either side.

The important thing is to be honest about which bucket you fall in, pursue that path, and then manage the situation without letting the mommy trolls or career warriors get in your way. Just remember, people who feel the need to criticize you are probably just insecure about their own situation, and making you feel like shit is the only way for them to feel better about their choices. We're all just doing our best out here. We know that doesn't make it easier to ignore, but you can either embrace that view or you can suffer. Your choice.

So let's say you don't want to go the mommy route, feel free to skip this section. But if you do, here's our advice on how to manage the maternity leave situation. Again, we have never been on maternity leave ourselves, so don't attack us (we already feel attacked). But based on our experience with employees going on maternity leave and friends who have taken leave, we have some opinions.

HOW TO DO THE BABY THING WITHOUT YOUR WHOLE OFFICE HATING YOU

As any mom will tell you, the maternity leave situation in America is pretty shitty compared to everywhere else in the developed world. However, there are definitely some positive things that you should be aware of, and the main thing to remember is that your employer is not allowed to fuck you over or discriminate against you because you're pregnant. If they do, document that shit and call a lawyer. Or maybe start by telling HR, and hopefully that will alleviate any grief people are giving you for your pregnancy or baby conflicts. But there's also some responsibility on you, if you want to be known as a cool mom and not an annoying mom.

Work at a place that supports mothers: Yes, we know we are privileged white girls who have had relatively easy lives in the socioeconomic sense, and not everyone has as many options as we do. Not everyone is blessed with a choice of where to work or financial room to make these types of decisions. However, if you are in a position where you have some sort of choice, and you know you're pretty likely to get pregnant in the near future, you should try to pick a job (or move to a new job) where the company is supportive of mothers and has good maternity policies. Do your research, read about it on Glassdoor, reach out to people who have worked there. You can ask in an interview what their policies are, but we can't promise they won't hold that question against you (even though it's illegal to do so, they still might take it into consideration), so either sandwich that question with curiosity about the company's other policies or find another route. Then make your decisions accordingly.

Communicate about your schedule: Obviously, having kids is going to mess with your schedule. They get sick, they have to go to school, whatever. While it's not possible to foresee every little issue and warn your employer, you should be as communicative as possible about the things you *can* control, giving as much notice as possible. Make sure your responsibilities are covered and your immediate coworkers are aware of when you will and won't be available. This is just one of the many annoying responsibilities that comes with being a mom, but it will definitely pay off in terms of people (or your child when they're old enough to bitch about you to their therapist) not thinking you're irresponsible.

Your baby is not always an excuse: Yes, your baby is an excuse a lot of the time, but we recommend never using him or her as an excuse unless he or she *truly* is the excuse. That's because you're probably going to have to switch up your schedule a lot due to your baby responsibilities anyway, and adding to that tab when it's not completely necessary is a bad idea. And this isn't because we hate babies, it's because people hate when their coworkers are irresponsible, regardless of whether a baby is the reason. So minimize the excuses, and people may end up really respecting your ability to juggle mom life and career life.

Don't foist your work onto coworkers: Ugh, just don't be the person who is constantly asking people to cover for her or literally do her work. This is even worse than using your baby as an excuse because you're asking people to take on your burden for you. It's better to take responsibility and ultimately complete your tasks (maybe late, or not as well) than it is to ask someone to literally do it for you.

Find a life partner who helps you: This could actually be one of the most important things in this book. This is not just important for childcare, but for life in general. Remember when you used to date fuckboys who wouldn't answer your texts and it would seriously stress you out, and you couldn't concentrate on anything or get through general life feeling okay? (Hopefully this is a distant memory and not a memory from a half hour ago.) Imagine that on a lifelong scale, except now this fuckboy is not only in a legal union whereby you own half of each other's shit, but you share a baby (or multiple babies, OMG) who you're currently traumatizing because neither one of you wants to take responsibility.

> Women will have achieved true equality when men share with them the responsibility of bringing up the next generation.
>
> —Ruth Bader Ginsburg

> If you wanna be my lover, you have got to give. Taking is too easy, but that's the way it is.
>
> —Spice Girls

If you choose to have a life partner, picking a caring one who understands and respects your desire to have a career while also being a mother, or who financially supports you (if they can) while you take time off work to raise your kids, is one of the most important factors that determines female success. The flip side is having someone who always puts himself first, never thinks about how to help you achieve your dreams, or even like, give you a five-minute break from all the things you're expected to do.

It's obvious that your spouse plays a huge role in parenting, but what is less frequently said is that who you choose to marry is one of the most important career decisions you'll make as well. Choose wisely, and set expectations for what each of you wants from each other solidly and frequently during the various phases of your relationship.

Inspirational Career Betch: Indra Nooyi

We need to come together, as corporations and as a society to support workers who are caring for young children, aging parents, or both.
—Indra Nooyi

Indra Nooyi was born in India, went to Yale, and moved her way up the ranks to become the CEO of PepsiCo from 2006 to 2018. In 2017, she was named the second Most Powerful Woman in Business by *Fortune*. Indra often talks about the trade-offs we make when we decide to become mothers and how that affects how ambitious we are able to be in the workforce. She's discussed how as she's gotten older she's learned that you'll never get back the opportunity to be with your kids while they're young before they become adults and then they have to be the ones making time for you. After learning and experiencing hardships in her years climbing the corporate ladder, Indra used her position of power to institute policies at PepsiCo that she wished she could have had as a younger mother.

As of 2017, she mandated that PepsiCo offer in-house childcare services for employees at their headquarters. She believes women shouldn't have to choose between being great parents and being great at their jobs. As she says, "That's just part of our larger effort to make sure we're supporting our working caregivers in every way we can and empowering people to build not just a career, but a life." As more women take positions of power, it's up to us to make the workplace a more comfortable and family-friendly environment to reflect our needs and the needs of women who don't have the same voices or power as we do.

TL;DR

If you get anything out of this chapter, we hope it's the realization that what you do outside of work can be just as critical for your career success as what you do in the office. Whether it's getting organized, taking time away from your job so you can do your job better later, or understanding your life priorities in a larger sense, it's really important to think about your career as a slice of the pie that is your life, and not to let it overtake the entire thing.

No matter how much people will broadcast the hustle, the truth is that your career is not benefited by being the only thing in your life. Not that you shouldn't hustle, but you should approach your hustle with intention rather than constantly spinning your wheels, and sometimes that means taking time off to regroup, reprioritize, and binge *The Office* on Netflix for the fifteenth time.

Dear Betches,

I have a career-related question. I am twenty-five and finished grad school with my master's last spring. I started working right away and loved it. Mid-June of last year my husband and I decided we felt ready to have a baby. I stopped taking the pill under the impression that it would take a while for my body/hormones to regulate after being on the pill for almost ten years (I had horrible periods and it made them more tolerable) because *everyone* said it would take a while to get pregnant after long-term use. PSA, it can happen very quickly.

When I first found out I was pregnant I immediately consulted the employee handbook to see what their maternity leave policy was (it was a small company and didn't have HR). It was the standard twelve-week unpaid leave. I told my boss/owner of the company that I was pregnant and when I was due, and everything seemed fine. When I was twenty-six weeks pregnant they changed their policy and no longer gave maternity leave and if I chose to take off time, my job was not guaranteed to still be there upon my return. They had fewer than fifty employees and therefore were not required to give maternity/medical leave. It was so fucked-up, if you ask me. It was handled horribly, and I was really upset by the whole thing, so I put in notice a couple of months later and quit a few weeks before I was due.

Fortunately, my husband makes a very good living and we don't have to worry about the financial aspect of all this. Flash-forward to now and I have a beautiful five-month-old little boy. I'm feeling ready to go back to work, but I'm unsure of how to address this extended leave in the job-hunting process. I've gotten so many mixed responses—some say briefly explain it in the cover letter, some say don't mention I'm a mom at all because that often puts you at a disadvantage, some say wait until the interview. So, my question is, how do you think an extended leave or gap of employment should be handled?

Sincerely,
New-Mom Betch

- - - - - - - - - - - - - -

Dear New-Mom Betch,

First of all, your old company sounds particularly shitty, so you should be happy to be out of there. While companies with fewer than fifty employees are not required to even guarantee you'll have a job after unpaid

maternity leave, most of them do anyway so they can attract great talent and because it's become pretty standard in the United States.

In terms of looking for a new job, you're lucky that you haven't been out of the workforce that long. Many times, moms have to deal with reentering the workforce after years of staying home with their kids and they have a much harder time. A lot of them fail to keep up with their old job skills and find it difficult to stay in touch with what's going on in their industries.

You definitely don't have to include anything about your children in a cover letter when applying for a new job. It's illegal for employers to ask you if you're pregnant or plan on having more children in interviews, so only bring up your past childcare leave if it's asked about. If the person interviewing you asks about your current unemployment, this is the time to put a great and true spin on what happened at your last job. You simply say that the previous company you worked for didn't value their employees that much and so after your maternity leave you decided to look for a job that was more family-friendly and where your skills and talents would be more respected. Stress that you're eager and excited to reenter the workforce and let them know how much you've kept up to date with everything going on in your industry.

Considering the terrible experience you had in your last job, you should be actively looking for new positions at companies that offer family-friendly policies anyway and that are happy to have working moms on their team and will sympathize with your past predicament. Don't seem defensive about being a new mom. Instead, show the interviewer that you're excited to be there. Above all, be confident. You were great at your job at your last position, and taking some time off to concentrate on your new family will rarely be a negative to any company you'd actually want to be a part of.

Good luck!
Betches

PS: Many women definitely get pregnant immediately after they stop taking birth control. Plan accordingly, betch.

Conclusion
LET'S CIRCLE BACK ON THIS LATER

Congrats, you've gotten through your first non-boring-as-shit career book. Sheryl Sandberg would be so proud. You're one step closer to figuring out WTF you want to do with the rest of your life.

Answers to all of life's existential questions aside, hopefully if nothing else, you've gained a few tips about proper punctuation in your résumé or learned how to not dress like a baby prostitute at the office. In all seriousness, we hope this book has given you the tips to not only master whatever dream career you're trying to pursue but to also help you think critically about why it is you even want to be doing that job in the first place.

Like anything else in life, self-actualization and figuring out how you want to support yourself aren't that straightforward. It doesn't happen overnight, and it's a process that will continue throughout your whole life. You're never going to read a book, have an epiphany, and magically fall into the career of your dreams. You have to figure out who you are in the first place, what makes you happy, and how much you're willing to sacrifice to get there. Yes, it sucks and that sounded so daunting that it made us want to take an Adderall immediately. But the good news is, now is the greatest time in the history of the world (so far) to be a woman in the workforce. You can literally try to be anything you want to be and there are thousands of tools you can use to help you get there. I mean, imagine how much Queen Elizabeth could've gotten done if she was equipped with a Venmo account and Microsoft Excel.

There's never been a better time to be a working mom, a female CEO, or even an amazing stay-at-home mom. Our forebetches fought for us to have the right to choose what we do all day and the legal rights to do it in a comfortable environment where we don't have to dodge sexual predators or domineering husbands. Shit isn't perfect, but at least there have been some improvements. We still have a ways to go in terms of complete equality, and we've only had the right to find fulfillment outside our homes for a short time on a world-history scale. There's a lot of catching up we have to do to make sure that what we deal with in our day-to-days at work is even easier for our future grandbetches.

Here's a little summary of WTF we've been talking about,

in case you passed out from boredom once you read the word *LinkedIn.*

- You have to figure out what you like to do *and* are skilled at, in order to find out what kind of job you should actually be pursuing. Something you enjoy doing that makes you no money is called a hobby, not a job.

- Get your shit together and follow the rules. You're not above making a great résumé and cover letter, and you have to actually put effort into things like going on interviews and researching companies.

- Once you have that job, don't mess it up by doing something stupid. Know how to present yourself in a professional way that makes you seem competent and prepared. When you prove yourself and work hard, make sure you're making the amount of money you deserve, and if you're not, find a job that values you.

- If you want to be your own boss, don't half-ass it. Despite how glamorous it looks in *Forbes*'s 30 Under 30, working for yourself actually takes a shit ton of sacrifice, so don't think you can reap the rewards of starting your own company/business/Instagram without having to suffer a little. It's not all as great as it looks on the #girlboss hashtag. So if you're going to go for it, whole-ass it.

- Remember that you live in the twenty-first century and everything you do is recorded, digitally stored, and can be used against you. Be careful how you present yourself online and do your best to keep your personal and work lives separate.

- Know that times are changing, and you have rights. Don't let men or anyone else make you feel like your sexuality has anything to do with your professional progress or discourage you from being ambitious.

- Finally, know when to check out. Work is important, but it's not everything. A whole, fulfilling life is one that prioritizes not only your career but also your friends, family, and hobbies. When you lie on your deathbed you won't regret the time you missed a meeting so that you could go to Cabo on a girls' trip. You'll regret wasting your energy at a job you hate that doesn't fulfill you or allow you to feel important and happy.

We hope this book has taught you the things that no one tells you in college, like that work can sometimes really suck, but when it's great, it makes you feel like you're leaving a legacy and really contributing to the growth and awesomeness of our society. Few things can feel as good as putting your blood, sweat, and tears into something and getting to see it succeed and help others and/or the world.

They say you can't have it all but like, fuck them. They might be right, but just like that time you blacked out and ordered two pizzas for yourself, you certainly can and should try to have as much of it as humanly possible. Your dream career isn't going to show up at your doorway begging for you to take it. So stop crying in the bathroom, get your shit together, and start updating your résumé. That glass ceiling isn't going to shatter itself.

Acknowledgments

We'd like to take another break from thinking about ourselves to thank everyone who helped us not only write this book but also build a company and careers we're proud of.

We want to give credit to our amazing team at Betches, who teach us something new every day and whose hard work and creativity entertains and empowers millions of people. You've taught us way more about running a business than any MBA program ever could. A special thank-you to Alise for her written contribution to this book, to Kenzie for her artwork, and to Brittany for the cover art.

To Kate and Alyssa, who believed in Betches from the start and continuously encourage us to get our shit together so that we could bestow the wisdom in this book upon the world.

To our partners, who listen patiently as we vent about work drama, lift us up, and believe in us and our success.

To our parents and family, who eventually came to accept and love the fact that we didn't become doctors and lawyers and instead pursued careers telling jokes on the internet. To our friends, who helped us build this company with their humor, stories, and personal anecdotes. To the late Sy Feit, in particular, who taught us the importance of organization and focus. To our financial and legal team, who protect us and urge us to do boring shit like pay taxes and get insurance.

And finally, to our incredible fans and loyal followers, who have kept us in business and who learn and laugh with us every day, allowing us to have the greatest jobs in the world. If we weren't as fucked up as you are, we wouldn't be able to relate to you in our writing, memes, and podcasts on a daily basis, and for that we are eternally grateful.